Andrew Wetmore

The Red Shift

Five short plays

An evening's entertainment

Cover design: Rebekah Wetmore

ISBN: 978-1-990187-34-6
First edition October 2022

2475 Perotte Road
Annapolis County, NS
B0S 1A0

moosehousepress.com
info@moosehousepress.com

We live and work in Mi'kma'ki, the ancestral and unceded territory of the Mi'kmaw People. This territory is covered by the "Treaties of Peace and Friendship" which Mi'kmaw and Wolastoqiyik (Maliseet) People first signed with the British Crown in 1725. The treaties did not deal with surrender of lands and resources but in fact recognized Mi'kmaq and Wolastoqiyik (Maliseet) title and established the rules for what was to be an ongoing relationship between nations. We are all Treaty people.

Production rights

The copyright for the plays in this book belongs to the author. In buying this book you get the enjoyment of putting on the plays in the theatre inside your head, as you read them.

If you want to perform these scripts in any way, including as staged readings for a non-paying audience, as an audio play, or as an amateur or professional live or recorded production, you **must** obtain permission in writing from the author or their representative. To do otherwise is a violation of copyright and not a nice thing to do to another theatre person.

For information about royalties and obtaining performance rights, send an email to info@moosehousepress.com. We will forward serious inquiries to the author.

Also by Andrew Wetmore

Shakescenes: four plays for Shakespeare lovers

Just Add Actors: ready-to-serve short plays

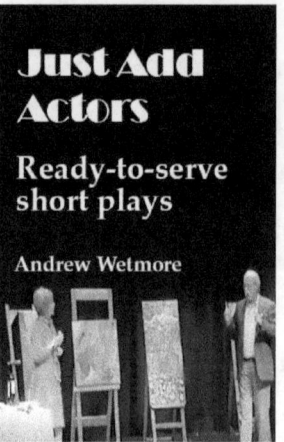

Both are available from moosehousepress.com

The turn of a phrase

One of the delights of working with a smaller production company, or a community theatre, is that everybody not only must, but willingly does, turn their hand to many tasks. The ticket-taker also manages the follow-spot. The head of makeup is also the prompter. The playwright helps paint the set.

So also with the actors. There is less health in a small company if those with big onstage roles consider other tasks beneath them. Without those other tasks, there would be no stage to perform on and no audience to see what you do. There is also less health in a company with one or two key actors who always get the juicy parts.

Having been a part of less-healthy theatre companies, I wanted Moveable Feast Theatre to give opportunities to many, without downgrading the quality of the show so far that the fun went out of being in the audience. I think that, over the company's time of activity (roughly, 1990-98), we achieved that. Some who started acting with MFT went on to careers on stage and in movies. Others became adept at lighting, sound, and costumes. At the same time, we grew a healthy audience base that even turned out for our more-experimental shows (ah, John Bowen's *Fall and Redemption*, in which eleven actors played more than 60 parts...).

At some point, while casting around for scripts that would provide a good range of parts for a wide range of actors, I decided to write a series of loosely-connected short plays that would make up an evening's entertainment, with a cast of five. Each actor would have at least one juicy part, and could spread their wings by taking on several different characters in a single production. Each actor also had at least one 'time out' during the evening when they could catch their breath.

You hold the result in your hands. The thread connecting the five very different plays is the phrase 'the red shift'. Keep your eye and ear out for it.

I had the great pleasure of directing the first production of *The*

Red Shift with MFT; and the great honour of attending the show's first professional production. I have also learned that the individual plays stand up pretty well on their own. I have performed 'New York Artist' as part of a show with a dozen short plays by different authors, but one of my great regrets is that I have never been in the cast of a production of the other four plays.

And now: over to you. As you read the scripts, let them come to life in the theatre of your mind. Or get a few copies of the book, have four friends over, and do a table reading for learning and hilarity.

Or...dare I say it? I do: suggest to your local theatre group that they put on the full *Red Shift*[1]. I would love to hear how it goes.

Andrew Wetmore
September, 2022

---

1   See the page on 'production rights' near the front of the book

Cast assignments

If you are producing these plays as a single evening of theatre, as they were designed, you need at a minimum a cast of three men and two women. The plays work with nonbinary actors in some parts.

Actor 1 and Actress 1 are older, or can "play older".

The division of parts, for a cast of five, is as follows:

	Pre-morial	A New York Artist	About the Dress	Lucked	Swift-Tuttle
Actor 1	Statue	Matt		Red	Otto
Actor 2	Statue		Tony	Leroy	Marcus
Actor 3	Green	Assistant		Dwayne	Mike
Actress 1	Cowley		Deborah	Umpire	Chloe
Actress 2	Statue		Micheline	Becky	Daphne

To the actors and audiences of Moveable Feast Theater, which flourished in Western Massachusetts in the 1990s, creating unreasonably good productions on a shoestring.

The author has created the characters, conversations, interactions, and events in these plays, and any resemblance of any character to any real person is coincidental.

Contents

Andrew Wetmore

Premorial

A desk, two chairs. A door. COWLEY in a chair, working;
GREEN at the door.

COWLEY
Well, come in, come in. Don't stand there in the door like a—

GREEN
Yes. I'm sorry. I'm not sure if I'm in the correct place.

COWLEY
It's the correct place for me. What it is for you depends on who you
are. Who are you?

GREEN
Green. David Green.

COWLEY
Oh, Mr Green David Green. Then it may well be the right place for
you, also, Mr Green. Come further in, Mr Green, if you dare.

GREEN
—If I dare?

COWLEY
A figure of speech. We deal in figures and forms of speech here. In
government, the one who forms the speech can shape the world.
Do you find that statement treasonous, or merely true?

GREEN
I—

COWLEY
Or both?

GREEN
I haven't actually met a lot of world-shapers, um.

COWLEY
Come aboard, Mr Green. Draw near enough, and you can read the plaque on my desk. If you then conclude I am at the desk allotted to me, you may know better whether this is a good place for you to be found in. You may prefer this to bending toward me to read the tag I wear on my...chest.

GREEN
I have an appointment.

COWLEY
So begins many a sad story. With whom?

GREEN
With you. That is, with...well, I had thought it was a *Mr* Cowley.

COWLEY
Don't let's be infantile. Let us set aside the puerile assumption that one holding the power to set you on high, or to crush you to a fine powder, must needs be a man.

GREEN
Not at all.

COWLEY
Not at all. Far from it. Heaven forbid. Oh, Mr Green, can I have misjudged you?

GREEN
I'm sorry. I could go out and come in again.

COWLEY
Do you but try. An utterly different person may await your return.
One even more cranky than I am. Cranky enough to make you
extremely blue, Mr Green.

GREEN
Then I think I'll stay.

COWLEY
Better the devil you know, Mr Green.

GREEN
But I don't know you, uh, Ms Cowley.

COWLEY
Clearly: it's *Doctor* Cowley.

GREEN
Doctor Cowley.

COWLEY
Honorary doctorate. Conveyed to impress me at a convocation just
this spring. It worked, Mr Green. I use it all the time and always
remember with gratitude my honorary alma mater. I send them
honorary donations, written in virtual ink. Now: my honorary alma
mater is in fact *thy* alma mater, Mr Green.

GREEN
Congratulations, Doctor.

COWLEY
Mmm. Do sit down, dear Mr Green. Perhaps over time we can

patch up your conversational gaffes, and achieve a dislike of each other based on more than superficialities. Mmm.

Green sits.

COWLEY
Now: although you know little of me, Mr Green, be assured I know much about you. Not all, though. Not yet.

GREEN
A little knowledge is a dangerous thing.

COWLEY
Dangerous to you, assuredly.

They regard each other for a moment.

GREEN
I'm sorry, I seem to be wasting your time and irritating you to no purpose. I don't want to keep you from your work—

COWLEY
You are my work of the moment, Mr Green.

GREEN
Then let's get on with it.

COWLEY
I am getting on with it, Mr Green. No moss grows on me. For an artist, you seem a great bundle of inattention.

GREEN
I can pay attention.

COWLEY
Do so, then. You see before you a being such as yourself, with lips

that part moistly to say, ah-ha. You note a body of such a weight, Mr Green, and such a combination of limbs and organs that it is as analogous to yours as a nut may be to a bolt. So, having paid that much attention, you think you know all. You have me figured out, Mr Green. You have seen through me as far as you care to look.

GREEN
With respect, that's nonsense. I am, in fact, brim-level with a healthy curiosity that has nothing to do with the, um, nuts and bolts of human relations.

COWLEY
Good.

GREEN
You called me here, and I'm sure it wasn't in order to discuss our college. I presume you drew me here because of some project or other in which I could be of assistance. An inventory of my skills suggests the project will have to do either with sculpture or with the making of lime mayonnaise, the two areas in which I have something to offer.

COWLEY
Oh, very good.

GREEN
So which is it to be, Dr Cowley? A new instant salad-dressing for our fighting forces? I warn you, I charge dearly for my culinary secrets.

COWLEY
My dear boy, if you had secrets, and we wanted them, we would have them out of you in a flash. And you would no longer feel the slightest interest in the amount of your remuneration. Thank your lucky stars you have no secrets.

GREEN
I—

COWLEY
We know. We checked.

> *Green rises, starts to speak.*

COWLEY
Should I rise also, or is this to be a self-righteous denunciation before you storm out and slam the door?

> *Green crosses to the door.*

COWLEY
The door won't open until I open it.

> *Green checks the door. Turns and faces her.*

COWLEY
Now sit down, silly man. There is an exit from this room festooned with wealth and honour, but you will not bluster your way through it.

> *Green sits again.*

COWLEY
Thank you. All the truly frightening branches of our government are housed in other buildings, so stop swivelling your eyes about. Now: our sharing of a college is germane, because through it I heard of you. As I was told, and as I saw while walking about the campus before convocation began, you evidently have talent in the making of monumental art. You will doubtless be famous after your untimely death by malnutrition for the subtlety and strength of your works. Would you, I wonder, care to be famous this side of the grave? Would you enjoy possessing the means and the

opportunity to design more than your own headstone?

GREEN
I—

COWLEY
These are of course rhetorical questions. Without commissions from institutions with more money than sense, your monumental wonders will never grow from your charming clay models and your little campus installations into anything you would wish the real world to see.

GREEN
I will get commissions.

COWLEY
You have to borrow the stamps with which to correspond with your potential patrons. You will soon have no telephone upon which to call them. But never fear. I have a commission, as it happens, ripe to fall from my outstretched hand into yours. Would you like to hear about it?

GREEN
Not mayonnaise, then?

COWLEY
No. Stone or steel, I fancy; or one of the new alloys.

GREEN
What is it?

COWLEY
We don't know. We are not artists.

GREEN
I mean, what is it for?

COWLEY

Morale. Posterity. Beyond that, it is a commission which will make your bank clerk break into a fine sweat when you deposit it.

The matter is this: we need a war memorial, one which can be ready to bolster national pride at a moment's notice. One a grieving but triumphant government can unveil at a ceremony which brings together the hearts and wills of all our survivors— and may they be many.

We have known this need for some time, and have had a sequence of plans on file, ready to roll out as soon as the all-clear sounded. Some of the proposed works were really super, really touching. Brought a tear to my eye. But nothing, I assure you, to touch what I believe you could accomplish.

Unfortunately, our dear old friends the Soviets have let us down. The Reds have shifted, ho-ho. They are no longer our fierce foes, dedicated to overthrowing capitalism. No, they have embraced capitalism with an obscene intimacy, and how can we now set them up as the ultimate enemy. Their oligarchs look and act like ours.

Their successor states are worth watching, of course, but they are often more concerned with fighting each other than with fighting us. In short, "the Reds" are not the threat they once were.

It is in principle a situation I applaud. It had occurred to us to wonder whether there would be a sufficient quantity of survivors to produce a really nifty war memorial, following a spasm of mutual assured destruction.

But we now face a much more subtle crisis, Mr Green. A crisis which will not swamp the ship of state, but which bids fair to peel off from it such barnacles as are you and I.

GREEN

I don't follow you.

COWLEY

Then you will arrive nowhere. Where are you lost?

GREEN
If I knew that, I wouldn't be lost.

COWLEY
You think not? I am beginning to suspect, Mr Green, that you were born in a condition of dis-location; and that unless you are taken in hand you will wander without purpose to a premature dissolution. Focus. Concentrate.

GREEN
(after a moment)
So you're saying, if there's no more war, there'll be no more monuments.

COWLEY
There will always be more war. Bank on it. Bet your life on it.

GREEN
So you're saying...what are you saying?

COWLEY
If the choice was between making fine art and entering a skilled profession, I think you chose well, Mr Green. You exhibit the reasoning powers of an easel.
  There will be more war; there will be more monuments. But we have no idea what sort of monuments there will need to be. Whom are we to defeat? What iconography will be available to represent the fallen foe? Which direction will it face: east, west...south?

GREEN
Won't it be obvious once the war is over?

COWLEY
"Once the war is over" will be far too late. Surely I don't need to tell you how long it takes to plan and execute a great work. We cannot

afford to let a monumental gap develop between the execution of the deeds and their commemoration. Ideally, the eternal flame should be lit from the embers of a defeated city.

This then is our challenge: the directive has come down on high to secure a design for a monument that will express perfectly, and on a moment's notice, the spirit of the war we have not yet fought. Its designer will receive a handsome reward.

GREEN
And you want me to do this?

COWLEY
A true patriot would hardly pause to be astonished.

GREEN
I am overcome.

COWLEY
Don't bask in the warm golden glow quite yet. We don't want you to do it unless you *can* do it. Can you?

GREEN
...Yes. Yes.

COWLEY
Good.

GREEN
Yes. I could do that, I think. I mean, I know I can—

COWLEY
Fine. Commendable. I knew it all the time.

> *Beat.*

COWLEY
What?

GREEN
What?

COWLEY
What? Will you do?

GREEN
Uh.

COWLEY
Have you not seized on the point that time is of the essence? Peace is raging wherever we look: we need now to prepare for its failure, in whatever quarter it comes.

GREEN
You want to know *now*?

COWLEY
I wanted to know yesterday.

GREEN
But...but...that's not how you create art!

COWLEY
We're not artists, so we could care less. What we have is a commission and a question whether you can satisfy it. A question mark against your name that is, I may say, growing.

GREEN
This is ridiculous.

COWLEY
This is government. Fish or cut bait, young man.

GREEN
Wait.

COWLEY
We are not unreasonable. We do not expect an absolutely finished product this very moment. But we do expect—

GREEN
Wait. Well...wait, do you have—?

COWLEY
(providing them
Paper, pencil, straight edge, kneadable eraser—though of course I trust you will not be *needing* that, ho, ho.

GREEN
Yes. No.

> *He picks up the a pencil.*

COWLEY
If you prefer, you can use a drawing app—

GREEN
(starting to draw)
No. Hush.

> *Cowley opens her mouth to speak, thinks better of it.*
> *As Green scribbles each idea, it starts to form behind him in the bodies of the three other actors.*

GREEN
Size is no object, right?

COWLEY
Size, material, style—all you have to do is please us, and we will

provide what you need. We will frown on literal eternal flames, of course, as they would involve an ongoing expense. We want this thing to be profound and durable.

GREEN
No eternal flame?

COWLEY
Minimal maintenance brings smiles to those on high.

GREEN
Okay. Okay. How about something joyfully triumphant, in the style of Madame Liberty at the barricades?

> *He shoves the paper at Cowley. ACTORS ENTER and form an upward fountain of arms in support of the central woman.*

COWLEY
If we wanted a French monument we would buy one. Besides, what if they are the enemy? It would be rude.

GREEN
France might be the enemy?

COWLEY
The identity of the enemy is our business. Only the war memorial is yours.

GREEN
Well...

COWLEY
And, of course, keep away from distinguishing national characteristics of the defeated. France is our ally at the moment, and may be again. A monument which stigmatizes a future friend will not have a future itself.

GREEN
(drawing rapidly)
Um...how about an act of magnanimity toward a fallen foe?

> *A man offers his hand to the woman, who is in a ditch, while the other man covers them with a weapon.*

COWLEY
Oh, yes. The Nazis had a poster like this in Belgium. Storm trooper helping a little boy out of a ditch. People scrawled on it, "Why did you knock him down in the first place?" Hmm: no. Besides, we won't be feeling magnanimous when this thing goes up.

GREEN
Would you prefer it without people? A slab...

> *The three make a ladder out of their arms, like a list of names.*

COWLEY
We have one of those. It's very touching, all those rows and rows of names of our people who died. The sons and daughters we lost. It is not about victory, Mr Green. It reinforces thoughts of the futility and waste of war, of sorrow, of regret, of shame, of mortality. Of voting for an opposition party. Oh, yes: another "victory", another memorial like that and the whole nation will sink into a quivering, shared melancholia. Up-beat, Mr Green: up-beat is what we want.

GREEN
Not figures, then.
(scribbling)
Not names. Something, something like maybe a stone eternal flame.

> *He shoves the sheet across the table. The actors form a flame.*

COWLEY
Looks like an exploded artichoke.

GREEN
It's just a first sketch!

COWLEY
Boring.

GREEN
Then we can use chromatizing polymers! Lacerated prismation
Aeolian effects!

COWLEY
And if the Aeolians are the enemy?

GREEN
Aeolus was the Greek god of the winds.

COWLEY
(this is news)
Ah, yes.

GREEN
Wind harps!

The actor-statue begins to hum and thrum.

GREEN
Hollows and tubes and junctures which pulse according to the
wind, making an eternal hymn, a chorus that will last as long as the
wind itself; the very breath of the nation, thrumming through the
hollows and interstices of the installation will generate a
harmonious and affecting chord—no, a series of chords: I'm sure it
could be made to do that...

They listen for a moment.

COWLEY
This has a certain ring...

GREEN
It's beautiful! Never the same, but with elusive themes that
evolve...

COWLEY
What does it remind me of?

GREEN
It's your heart singing, singing with love for those who died and
those who survived, with love for this country. That's what you
hear.

They listen.

COWLEY
Whales.

GREEN
Wales is the enemy? It doesn't even have its own army.

COWLEY
No: the sound. That's what those whales sing to each other. Not
Welshmen. Seagoing mammals.

They listen.

GREEN
Surely not.

COWLEY
That's exactly what it is. Whale songs. You've designed us a
memorial to the Battle of Nantucket. The Victory Over Blubber.

The actors stop humming.

GREEN
You don't like it?

COWLEY
If you placed it in a garden would it keep away predators?

GREEN
(after a moment)
You don't know what you want. You just want to not want. You
want to negate, to tear down. You brought me in here to humiliate
me—

COWLEY
Not at all.

GREEN
This is all a sham. You don't want anything that an artist can give
you. You want just a monument to yourself. A tribute to those who
take no risks, take no stand, take nothing but their salary.

Actors form a desk, a chair, a seated bureaucrat.

GREEN
Well, maybe you're right. Yes, I'm sure you're right. After all, if
there is another war—

COWLEY
When there is another war—

GREEN
—who will be left at the end of it? Who will be able to protect themselves? Not the whales, not the soldiers, certainly not the artists: just you and the cockroaches!

COWLEY
Do you always malign others when you fail at a task?
GREEN
Who am I to design a war memorial? All I know is art. I've never even fired a gun! Or are you afraid to ask somebody who knows something about war?

> *Actors form a tableau of horror.*

GREEN
What sort of design would a soldier show you? What would he want to look at? What would he want to remember of himself in war, once it was over?

> *Actors form a tableau of grief.*

GREEN
Who goes and looks at a war memorial, anyway? Ask the widows and motherless sons what it should look like.

> *Actors form a tableau of wounded warriors.*

GREEN
Ask them: go on. Then have me back in, me or somebody else, and let us talk to the soldiers and the widows and then see what we can do.

> *A beat. Then the actors melt down out of sight.*

COWLEY
Yes. Well, thank you for that inspirational sermon, Mr Green. This

interview is at an end.

GREEN
I could do it then: I know I could.

COWLEY
(standing)
Thank you.

> Pause. Then GREEN goes to the door and opens it.

GREEN
So, then...about the commission?

COWLEY
I'll make you a deal, Mr Green: don't call us, and we won't call you.

GREEN
All right. I'm sorry if I spoke out of turn just then—

COWLEY
No need to shut the door. It will close behind you.

> Pause. Then Green EXITS.
> Cowley sits. Pushes a button on a device on her desk.

COWLEY
Stop sniggering now: he was earnest, at least. Keep the bit about
whales, and cut to the farewells. Log it and file it for the director.
That bit about the whale songs was rather good.
    Add this cover memo: "To the director: We have now completed
106 artist interviews for Project Remember, in accordance with
the project plan outline, first stage, pre-design phase. We are
approaching the point where we will have sufficient subjective
data with which to begin to define the parameters of difficulty and
enter the project plan outline, first stage, design phase of this

project. Cost over-runs may necessitate a further disbursement from central funds. It is not possible as yet to project a date by which this work will be completed."

Good. Now send in the next one. Tell the others to come back tomorrow.

Blackout

A New York Artist

There is a chair SC. To one side are boxes full of books with red covers. On the other side are empty boxes.

MATT ENTERS. He is wearing a coverall on the shoulder of which is a red badge. He align the chair carefully until he is satisfied, and then sits.

WHISTLE blows. The ASSISTANT, in a coverall with a red badge, bustles in L with two boxes held high in front of him, and sets one down on each side of the chair. One box is empty; the second is full of books in red bindings. The Assistant EXITS L, looking at his watch.

Matt adjusts himself, the chair, and the boxes in the manner of a concert pianist. Then he puts his hands on his knees and speaks to the audience.

MATT
Losing that first job was for the best. It really was. I mean, when you come right down to it, it was an unhealthy environment and a beast of a boss, and who can thrive in those circumstances? And it was the sort of work where the fascination and the excitement dimmed very quickly.

He takes a book from the box, rips its cover off, puts the cover in the empty box and the pages back in the full box. He continues as he talks until he is out of books; then he rests his hands on his knees and continues to talk to the audience.

33

MATT

I know they never promised that an MFA in painting would mean
we could live as painters. They told all of us that only a few make it
big in art, and those few suck up all the air and all the reviews in
the magazines and all the walls in the best galleries. They told us, if
you don't have that special magic that will let you dare to be great,
why even try? They told us that the best we could hope for was to
teach. To teach others so the best of them would get jobs teaching
others, so the best of them would get jobs teaching others.

And I thought, these are the people who could not make it big in
the art world, telling me I cannot make it big in the art world. What
do they know? They didn't make it big!

Don't misunderstand me: Painting is what I wanted to do—
creating, making...taking in the world and breathing it out again on
canvas so people would say, "Oh, look: now I see the world in a
new way, because I have seen that painting."

That was my point. Not to make it big. To make a difference. But if
making it big was part of the cost of being a painter, I was resigned
to making it big.

So I took that job when it came up, even though it was in New
York, and even though I would then have to admit I had become a
New York Painter within two years of leaving college. Of course,
when people say, "New York Painter", they really mean about two
hundred people out of all the millions in the city, and I do believe
there are many more than that, even on Manhattan, who are
painters and I don't mean house. But the two hundred are all that
count.

Now I know it was for the best that job didn't last long. The
atelier was a broad room with many skylights facing north—north
light forever!—and there were rows and rows of us.

I tried to think sometimes what sort of factory it might have
been, what weary immigrant people sat under those skylights and
filed the flashings off gears, or sewed the binding on blankets.

People just like me.

Our job was to turn out paintings, paintings actual people would
actually buy. "Handpainted originals" real people could afford to

buy and hang on their walls, and their neighbours wouldn't think they'd gotten all high-brow and weird. So we painted them, and the boss distributed them; and we got paid and the boss made money and lots of folks got to look at real paintings on their walls. There are worse things to do with your day.

Did you know there were trends in wall art? Maybe you *do* know this, since after all you live where there are walls. Maybe you yourself have one—more than one!—sweet orphan child with huge eyes on a velvet background. And when you bought it, it seemed like the most original and fitting thing. And then one day you look at it and say, euwh. What was wrong with me when I brought *that* home? I need to take that down and give it to some charity auction and go out and buy a painting of a lighthouse!

Our boss's job was to stay one trend ahead of you, and to have the bowl of fruit with the wine bottle ready when it's time for the lighthouse to go. I don't know how he did it, but he did.

That was the real art of the business. What we painters contributed was small. You see, the paintings were pre-printed. Our job was to add enough "hand-painting" that people could come up real close and squint their eyes and see real, actual ridges and globbets and blends of real actual paint, and be assured it was a real hand-painted painting.

The owners of the paintings would not do that, but their dinner guests would, when the hosts were in the kitchen, and we owed it to our customers to allow them to look good.

I was on the red shift, which suited me fine. There is an awful lot you can do with red that the greens and the blues are never allowed. You can do ardour, they can do flu. You can do fury, they can do fear. You can do blood, they can do phlegm.

I took to it like a duck to orange sauce. Add a little red here, a little carmine there, a sunsety blend over here; then pass the painting to the blue shift and turn to the next one. I learned to be quick and accurate.

And then after a while I was so quick and accurate that I would get ahead of what the blue shift could handle. Then I would have time to look at the canvas, to add just a touch here and there—to get involved in it.

It was like a game to insert surprises in the painting, little secrets that would reward the careful viewer.

We were working on these Maud Lewis woodland scenes, and I found this stump back to the right, and with a couple of careful touches of red and magenta I could turn it into a man in a hunting jacket. A man lurking so as not to be seen. A man lurking, with the sun glinting off his rifle barrel....

This was so cool. I could imagine the painting's owner gazing at his rectangle of art months or years after he bought it, filling an idle moment...and then squinting a little, tilting his head: could I be seeing what I'm seeing?

There was a country town scene, very peaceful at the end of the day. I added just a touch here and there to the windows and the porch of one house, little tongues of red not even the occupants of the house would have noticed yet—but any moment someone would cry *Fire!*

> *WHISTLE blows. Assistant bustles in L with two new boxes, arranged as before. Inspects the first pair of boxes dubiously, then bustles off L with them.*

MATT

The only trouble was that nobody seemed to notice. I never heard from the owners if they saw my little gifts—well, of course not, because they had no idea we existed at our long tables under the skylights. But I wanted to share the fun of it. I wanted someone to be delighted as I was delighted. I am, above all, an artist.

So one day I told the nearest blue shift guy what I was doing. I thought maybe I could even inspire him to experiments of his own.

But he went and told the boss and the boss came and looked, and he took me by the upper arm and walked me out the door and that was that. Everybody's a critic.

That was a dry time. I found that I had been painting into the work of others for so long that I couldn't start with just a blank canvas. There was nothing to react to—no, there was the whole world to react to, but I had lost the means to react. I was no longer a New York painter. I was a New York nothing.

But, in the end, I think it was good I lost that job. It meant I was available for this one. And this job has its charms.

I work for this guy who makes fancy notepaper, incredible stuff. Some of it has seaweed, flowers, little bits of whatever that you can see on the page like its a piece of the world served up for you to write on. People love it.

Some of it has gum wrappers, ticket stubs, little bits of urban junk processed with the same reverent attention as if they were so much silk. The junque paper—that's j-u-n-q-u-e—has a market among urban folks and lovers of modern art. They tend to buy single sheets and frame them in expensive frames and discuss them with their guests during long evenings involving imported beer.

I'm working on the latest project now. I gave the boss this idea: paper that has already been used for the printing of ideas, recycled for writers. I said, you could sell the spirit of Hemingway, the spirit of Balzac—it's right there in the fibres of the paper, waiting to give energy to your new words, spirit to your stories.

Stands and looks out each wing. Sits again.

MATT
(conspiratorially)
I have to tell you I suggested it in the spirit of putting the gunman among the trees of the Maud Lewis painting. Just for fun, really; just to see what would happen. And he got this look in his eye, and he said, "Great idea!", and I'm thinking, boy, is he going to be pissed when this bombs.

But people love it. He has sold a ton. I think people buy reams of this paper to give to their friends who are writers, and the friends who are writers say, "Whoa: neat idea!" and then the friends buy them some more.

I don't know if the writers ever actually use it, or if it makes a difference to their writing; but I suppose if they believe it does, it does.

I'm on the red shift again, as you can see. Covers true reds, deep browns, ochres...everything through orange and into purple. We have a room and a team for almost any color you can mention. Preparing the books, trashing the covers because the machines can't handle them, turning them into writers' paper. The paper is so popular, we can hardly keep up.

For me, that's where the problem comes in. It was my own silly idea, but once the boss got it going and people began to buy the paper, I guess I began to believe in it. I *do* believe in it.

> *Flourishes a book.*

MATT
So the quality of material I have to work with is beginning to get on my nerves. It was really exciting when we started, and we had rich mines of surplus Camus and William James and Margaret Atwood to work with. I really enjoyed bringing those guys into the process. But we need more and more books, always more.

And the standards go down and down. Norman Mailer, Kingsley Amis, okay. But Jacqueline Suzanne! Dame this and that fruity English mystery writer! I'm embarrassed to have them pass through my hands.

> *Rips the book apart.*

MATT
Every day we have to run a little faster. Where will it all end?

> *Deposits cover in its box, pages in other box. Stands and carries the chair L, places it carefully. puts the two boxes on top of the chair.*

MATT
If things were as they used to be, I wouldn't mind if this job lasted forever. I'm getting great muscles in my shoulders. But I am above

all an artist. I think that means that when I sell out, I want to sell out on my own terms.

Crosses C.

MATT
I've heard about this job in the food industry. It's the people who make that little chocolate candy with the colourful outer shell. They need a balance coordinator, someone who makes sure that there are enough candies of each colour in each package. I think I have special gifts I could bring to that job, so if this one goes down, I'm going to check it out.

Crosses R, taking a whistle out of his pocket.

MATT
I bought one of those bags of candy the other day, and I can see they need help. Lots of help. There were ninety-seven candies in the bag, and in the one I bought, only two were red. Only two red. (shakes head in dismay)
I think I could bring them a better balance than that. I know I could.

Matt BLOWS WHISTLE, then EXITS R. The Assistant ENTERS L, crashes into the chair and boxes. Looks around in bewilderment.

Blackout

About the Dress

A railed balcony, with a laundry line extending offstage from a post at the corner of the balcony. A hanging plant in full bloom is attached to the post by a bracket.

MICHELINE is sitting awkwardly DLC, half-out of a lawn chair (chaise longue type): her feet are on the floor, her arms are braced against the chair on each side of her as if she were about to jump up, and she is staring down   at her own chest. She is wearing a bikini. There is a diary tumbled to the floor beside her, lying beside a towel, a glass, and a bottle of lotion. Another lawn chair DR, with a light table or cart beside it.

MICHELINE
(under her breath)
Oh, go away. Go away go away go away go away...Please go away.

Then there is a scuffling sound and a hand appears on the balcony rail. TONY clambers into view: it is a difficult climb. He is wearing a light summer suit.

MICHELINE
Deb? Is that you? Don't come near me!...Deb?

Tony steadies himself, straddling the rail. He looks at Micheline, then out along the laundry line.

MICHELINE
Walk real light, okay? Talk real soft. Or just go away for now.

     Beat.

MICHELINE
Deb?

TONY
Hello. Hello, yes. It's a lovely day, and although the circumstances are a little unusual in which we meet, I dare hope that, when we look back on them later, we will find them to have been auspicious.

MICHELINE
Who the hell are you?

TONY
I'm—

MICHELINE
Where are you? What are you doing?

TONY
I'm right here behind you.

MICHELINE
Go away!
(to her chest, softer)
Go away.

TONY
I have only just arrived. Not really arrived, in fact. If you turn around, you would see that I have only trespassed onto your balcony to the depth of the width of one foot.

MICHELINE
I can't turn around. Go away.

TONY
I understand your chagrin at being saluted from an unexpected
direction, in the midst of your meditations. And I understand that,
although I have only intruded this foot-width, uninvited entry, of
even the slightest measurement, is, well, uninvited.
   However, I am faced with a difficulty. I have tried to resolve it, in
my mind, with a variety of strategies. And, do you know, this one
seemed, despite its awkwardness, the one least likely to cause you
distress.

MICHELINE
Who are you?

TONY
I am sorry: my name is Tony.

> *He holds out his hand toward her; she of course does not*
> *respond. He drops his hand.*

TONY
It is so difficult to meet people nowadays. And even more difficult
when one, after all, wishes to meet a particular person, rather than
people in the generality.

MICHELINE
(strained whisper toward the rest of the apartment
Deb! Deborah!
(to Tony) There are other people here, so why don't you—?

TONY
Then I will meet both a specificity and a generality of people: my
lucky day.

MICHELINE
Listen, whoever you are—

TONY
Tony.

MICHELINE
Tony: I am busy just now. So why don't you just take your foot off my balcony and go back to wherever you came from?

TONY
With the deepest respect, I would like to put aside your suggestion. In the first place, it took the gravest, most exalted motivation to bring me up here, for I am afraid of heights. In the second place, this compulsion which has given me the courage with which to climb will not permit me the coldness of heart with which to depart, until I achieve my goal.

MICHELINE
Are you out of your mind?

TONY
I think not: no. Not in the sense you mean.

MICHELINE
I can't talk to you now—I'm busy!

TONY
I also was busy, busily on my way as I walked along your street below. So far below...But there are certain imperatives in the face of which all busyness must be suspended. I hope you will agree that this is such a case, and pause in your deliberations long enough to hear me, as I in my turn have broken my journey in order to climb to your balcony.

MICHELINE
A salesman, right?

TONY
Oh, no.

MICHELINE
A missionary.

TONY
Not exactly.

MICHELINE
Do I owe you money?

TONY
You owe me nothing. I am in your debt.

MICHELINE
I can't do this right now, Terry.

TONY
Tony.

MICHELINE
Tony. Not now. Please, not now.

TONY
I could wait...

> *He brings his other foot over the rail.*

MICHELINE
No! I want you to go away!

TONY
There is no need to be afraid.

MICHELINE
Yes, there is.

TONY
The situation calls forth awe and wonder. Amazement. Delight. But not fear. In the end, not fear.

MICHELINE
Tony, I am thinking right now about pain and discomfort. I am associating these things in my mind with you. Is that what you want?

TONY
Naturally not.

MICHELINE
Then go away.

TONY
I will come no closer: will that do? Not until I am invited.

     Micheline groans.

TONY
From this reassuring distance, I will contemplate the muscles of your back. I will note that your vertebrae are a miracle, that the tone of your skin is like honey and the places where your hair brushes your shoulders are a song. There is no part of you that I can see in which I do not delight. Where in that could you possibly encounter pain and discomfort?

MICHELINE
This has nothing to do with you!

TONY
Then you cannot associate these negative things with me! You have
been pulling my leg!—a beguiling sensation, I might add.

MICHELINE
That's it!

> *She starts to stand up, still staring at her chest; then freezes,
> and slowly subsides.*

TONY
That's it? What was what?

MICHELINE
(to herself)
That was close.

TONY
Have you possibly disordered your back? It looks well from here,
but looks are not always everything.

MICHELINE
I'm not talking to you!

TONY
Oh, you deal in contradictions! You talk to me to tell me you are not
talking to me...I knew the subtlety of your mind, its playful
brilliance, before ever I began to climb. I knew the beauty of your
back and shoulders before ever I saw them. I knew the fine texture
of your skin, although it is beginning to redden in the sun—

MICHELINE
Shut up; just shut up.

TONY
And I have not seen your face; but even should it be less

profoundly wonderful than are your other attributes, I will be content.

MICHELINE
My face is none of your business, my back is none of your business, and my balcony is none of—oh!

She tenses, and then relaxes a little.

TONY
This was my opinion, too, until a very few minutes ago. I had not a thought of you, I did not know I had a need of you, until I glanced up at the sky and you beckoned to me.

MICHELINE
I did not!

TONY
Not in so many gestures, perhaps. But your beckoning was as eloquent and as tangible as if...as if... as if you had wrapped me up in a dictionary.

MICHELINE
I didn't do a thing. I haven't moved since—what did I do?

TONY
Your dress spoke for you.

MICHELINE
My dress?

TONY
Your dress, your frock, your shift, your gown—a whatever you wish to call it. I prefer "shift", myself. It is a slightly obsolete, slightly mysterious and medieval usage of the word. Your shift. It bears within itself a sense of rooms lit by candles and heavy with

shadows, of the silky material sliding over those shoulders, moving against that skin...

MICHELINE
I'm not wearing a dress!

TONY
I know: I'm not blind!

MICHELINE
Oh, good.

TONY
(pointing along the laundry line)
It hangs there on the line, your shift.

MICHELINE
It does?

TONY
It is red, a gentle but hot red. A carefree, amazing red.

Micheline turns her head slightly to look.

MICHELINE
Oh. That old thing.

TONY
As I turned the corner, I saw it. As I drew closer, the sun caught it. It undulated on the breeze. I was transfixed, and then impelled.
   You should understand that I am not a man who lacks. I have my home, my work, my ordinary pleasures. God has blessed me with a sweet life, in which I have done some good and less harm, in which I have glimpsed wonders and have caused mirth. Even, once or twice, applause. I have learned enough to understand that I am neither a sage nor a fool.

It is a life in which I do not often find myself intruding onto ladies' balconies. I have many acquaintances, or I may say friends, who would welcome me onto their terraces, verandahs, and porches at almost any hour, on almost any pretext.

But your shift beckoned to me. Not lewdly—although I imagine that she who wore it could be lewd enough, and happy at it. It beckoned to a place in me where there is no occupant.

I have friends, but no close friend, no friend of the heart. I have been intimate, but I have no love. Have had no love until now, I mean. It was a lack I had not lacked, and you have both identified it and filled it in one gesture of apparel.

I thought I had a purposeful and well-ordered life, but you have shown me how, well, shiftless it has been.

MICHELINE
You like the dress?

TONY
Adore it. Live for it. Admire it. Isn't it amazing?

MICHELINE
It's just a dress.

TONY
Surely I must not be the first.

> *DEBORAH ENTERS. She is dressed casually in after-work shirt and jeans. She carries a drink.*

DEBORAH
Not the first? Sorry, sweetheart. You're far from her first.

MICHELINE
(not moving)
Deb! Oh, my God, Deb!

DEBORAH
Don't worry: I won't tell him everything. Just enough so he'll treat you with respect.

MICHELINE
Come here, quick!

TONY
But I already know everything. All that I need to know, at least. Except your name, dear lady.

DEBORAH
(crossing to Micheline)
Deborah. Deb is fine.

TONY
Tony.

DEBORAH
Charmed.
(to Micheline)
So where did you net this one?

MICHELINE
You've got to help me!

DEBORAH
He's not that big. You can take him on all by yourself, and still have time to do the dishes. It's your turn.

MICHELINE
Look.

> *Tony starts to move toward her.*

MICHELINE
Not you!

> *Tony stops.*

MICHELINE
Here.

DEBORAH
Where?

> *She leans in.*

MICHELINE
Down my front. Do you see it?

DEBORAH
I see both of them. And very fine specimens they are.

TONY
Oh, my.

MICHELINE
Deb, stop teasing!

DEBORAH
Who's teasing? It's the two wasps in your bra you want me to look at, right?

MICHELINE
There are *two*?

DEBORAH
Two that I can see. Wasps or hornets.

MICHELINE
Ohhhhhh—

DEBORAH
I wouldn't squirm like that.

MICHELINE
I've been sitting here for twenty minutes. My arms are getting tired.

DEBORAH
So what are they doing in there?

MICHELINE
I don't know. I was reading, and I fell asleep, and when I woke up there they were.

TONY
If you have been heated by the sun, they may have come to drink of your sweat.

MICHELINE
Eeyewh!

DEBORAH
(interested)
Really?

TONY
Oh, yes. But they will not drink much.

DEBORAH
(peering)
I don't think they're drinking.

TONY
Oh, no. Not now, not if they have been there twenty minutes. Unless they are getting thirsty a second time.

MICHELINE
Get them out of there!

DEBORAH
Not me. I'm allergic to stings. Are you?

MICHELINE
I don't know.

DEBORAH
One way to find out.

MICHELINE
Don't we have some kind of spray? That bug stuff in the kitchen?

TONY
I would not advise that. They will writhe as they die, and who can tell what might happen? And it would also be bad for the skin.

DEBORAH
Why don't you just flip up your top and let them go? I'm sure Tony wouldn't mind.

MICHELINE
I thought of that. I tried. If I start to move, they get—active. I can feel their wings. I can feel their feet...I can feel their breath.

DEBORAH
Well. This is a new one on me. Tony—do you know from bugs?

TONY
It is not my field, no.

DEBORAH
Too bad. you could be a hero.

TONY
(rubbing his hands)
What requires to be done?

MICHELINE
No, no!

TONY
(crossing to her)
I would do anything that would grace and comfort your life.

MICHELINE
I'm fine: go away.

DEBORAH
Did you guys have a fight?

TONY
Not yet.

MICHELINE
I don't even know who he is!

TONY and DEBORAH
Tony.

TONY
Thank you.

DEBORAH
My pleasure.

>   *They consider each other.*

MICHELINE
Whatever you two are doing, go do it somewhere else.

DEBORAH
I might—but he's your friend.

MICHELINE
He's not my friend.

TONY
But I am endeavouring to become one, to become perhaps more than a friend. If I cannot assist in the matter of the wasps—

MICHELINE
You can't!

TONY
—then I can at least exhibit my friendship, my devotion, by pointing out that your back is becoming redder and redder, and that unless you take steps you may have great discomfort this evening.

DEBORAH
(looking)
You're right.
(to Micheline)
He's right.

MICHELINE
What do you expect me to do about it?

DEBORAH
Ask for help, perhaps. Nicely.

MICHELINE
So help, already.

DEBORAH
Tony, I believe Micheline requires your help.

MICHELINE
No—

TONY
I could stand between you and the sun to provide immediate and topical relief. Is that better?

MICHELINE
(reluctantly)
I guess so.

TONY
This will at least prevent additional harm. But the skin should be refreshed and protected. Is there a cream or a lotion?

MICHELINE
Uh-uh. No.

DEBORAH
Not on a first date?

MICHELINE
This isn't a date.

TONY
An encounter?

DEBORAH
A tryst?

MICHELINE
A nightmare.

DEBORAH
Oh, here's some lotion.

Squats down beside it.

MICHELINE
No, leave it. It's okay.

DEBORAH
How are your visitors?

MICHELINE
Just there. I can see their little stinger things.

DEBORAH
What if you slowly leaned forward, until they're standing on the bra instead of on you. Then Tony can kindly turn his back, and I can unhook the top, and you can shrug it off and we all run like hell.

MICHELINE
Do you think it would work?

DEBORAH
Do you?

MICHELINE
Well...

She slowly starts to lean forward. Then stops.

MICHELINE
Uh-uh.

Slowly returns to her previous position.

MICHELINE
Uh-uh, uh-uh.

TONY
Not what they desired?

MICHELINE
They were hanging on to me. And buzzing. They're quieter now.

DEBORAH
Maybe they don't like too much sun. Lotion for you.

She picks up the lotion and the book, and stands.

MICHELINE
I don't want you to. Don't bother. Oh—why is this happening to me?

TONY
Perhaps they are hoping to build a nest.

MICHELINE
Eeewww. Are these, are these the kind that make like a mud nest, so they'll have to go away and get stuff to make mud with? Or are these the kind that like dig a hole...?

TONY
May I look?

MICHELINE
No.

TONY
Then I cannot say.

DEBORAH
(of the book)
What's this doing here?

MICHELINE
(to the wasps)
Go away, you guys. Go find a drain pipe to sit in.

DEBORAH
Hey...

TONY
They must leave at some point, to seek food.

MICHELINE
That's true of people, too, right?

TONY
I am well sustained, thank you. No need to worry about me.

DEBORAH
This is my diary. What's it doing out here?

MICHELINE
Um.

DEBORAH
This never leaves my room. I never take it anywhere else. So how
did it get out here?

MICHELINE
Search me.

DEBORAH
You said you were reading. You were reading this?

MICHELINE
No. Oh, no. Never.

DEBORAH
(handing lotion to Tony)
Here: do her.

MICHELINE
Hey, wait.

DEBORAH
Tell me about the diary.

MICHELINE
I don't know anything about the diary. It was like just there when I sat down.

DEBORAH
You'll need to move those straps to do it right.

MICHELINE
What?

TONY
Oh, yes—of course.

He slides the straps off her shoulders.

MICHELINE
Okay. Okay. Okay.
(to Tony)
Don't jiggle me.

DEBORAH
So talk.

MICHELINE
(to Tony, as he starts on her back)
If you make those suckers sting me, you are going to be so sorry—

DEBORAH
I'm going to poke around in there with a stick if you don't start talking.

MICHELINE
Okay. All right.
(beat)
Okay, I was reading it. I was curious. I'm sorry. But you just kept hinting and bragging about all this wild stuff you do whenever you go out...I just wanted to see if it was true.

DEBORAH
That is so mean.

MICHELINE
Lying is mean, too.

DEBORAH
I never lied!

MICHELINE
What about the guy in the flower shop?

DEBORAH
Except for that.

MICHELINE
And Michael with all the tattoos?

DEBORAH
He had tattoos.

MICHELINE
He had one. On his left arm, and it says, "tattoo". You wrote it down
right there. He didn't have one like you told me, that thick snake
that you said slithered all around his hips and ended up—

DEBORAH
How dare you? How dare you steal my private property, and defile
it with your greasy thumbs, and then try to make me feel bad
about it?

MICHELINE
How dare you lie to me?

DEBORAH
(to Tomy)
Jiggle her.

MICHELINE
No, no!

TONY
And how are the insects?

MICHELINE
They're—they're—
(looks closer)
They're sort of—calm.

TONY
If you become calm as well, perhaps they will sleep. You have a
knot of tension just—here.

MICHELINE
No, don't make me—! Oh. Oh, that feels much better. What did you
do? It sent little sparkles down both my arms.

TONY
It is better not to be tense.

> *Presses at the base of her neck.*

MICHELINE
Ohh!...

> *She sags slightly and her head droops down.*

DEBORAH
(to Tony)
How can you touch her? She's a snivelling little sneak.

TONY
(to Deborah) It is better not to be tense.

DEBORAH
She doesn't deserve you. You let her into your life, and you'll regret it.

TONY
But she is already in my life. My life is captivated by her: by the way she moves, by her daring.

DEBORAH
Oh, yeah? And what does your wife think of her?

TONY
I was to marry, once. But she was not well; and then she died. Quite quietly, in her sleep. We knew it was likely and she was prepared. It was not a tragedy.

DEBORAH
That's so callous. How can you say that?

TONY
It was terrible, and I was very sad and lonely for a long, long time. But not a tragedy, no. If you live, eventually you meet death; and although she met him sooner than she would have chosen—well, that is a question of timing, not a tragedy.

DEBORAH
So she died and that was that? You just shrugged it off?

TONY
No. But I did not die with her.

DEBORAH
Oh.
(beat)
So, you're gay.

TONY
Oh, no, no. Only happy, now.

> *He slides his hands along Micheline's shoulders and down her arms to where the straps hang. She does not stir.*

DEBORAH
So where's the catch? What's wrong with you? I have looked very hard, Tony, and until this minute I would have said there were no single, straight, unkinky men over the age of 14 in this whole city. Are you out on bail?

TONY
I am sorry to disappoint you, and even more sorry that your luck has been so poor. I know myself how difficult it is to meet a person whom one would like to meet. Where is it that you search?

DEBORAH
Started with the bars. Then the health clubs, then continuing education classes. I found lots of nice married guys who wanted to take me out, lots of guys in recovery who wanted to tell me about their twelve steps. I joined a church, for crying out loud! I put a personal ad in the paper.

TONY
Forgive me, but perhaps your grace and attractiveness are daunting. Even the men who swagger and bluster are much more shy than they may seem. And the two of you together—!

DEBORAH
We're not together! We only share the apartment. She's the sister of a guy I knew a long time ago, and she looked me up when she moved to town, to just stay a while until she got settled. And it's been months. She could get her own place, but she's always got some excuse.

TONY
Perhaps she likes to stay because you are her friend.

DEBORAH
Is she asleep, or what?

TONY
For a little while. I relaxed the net of nerves that—

DEBORAH
Come here a second.

>   *Tony crosses to her.*

DEBORAH
When she first came she was like the country mouse, you know? But she's got this knack: she got a better job than I have, on her

first interview, she's working on some computer course at the college, she even knows the first name of the guy at the convenience store.

TONY
Arthur? Or Dwayne?

DEBORAH
I don't know! Both of them!...It's like she hardly even tries, and she's doing all the things I never succeed at. If the dj says be the third caller and win two tickets to this great concert, and she calls up, she's always the third caller. She used to think I was this big deal foxy lady that dumped her brother, and now it turns out she can do it all better than I can. That's why I make up stories about what I've been doing—

TONY
It is not my business.

DEBORAH
Cause if I told her really what I'm doing, I wouldn't have anything to tell her.

TONY
Surely it is better than that.

DEBORAH
I was beginning to think she wasn't even into guys, but I didn't really know how to ask her, and anyway I'd been spinning all these stories about my guys, and now here it turns out she has a guy.

TONY
It is my unexpected good fortune.

He crosses back to Micheline.

DEBORAH
Well, great.
(beat)
And I suppose she is, right?

TONY
She is—?

DEBORAH
Great. You know.

TONY
Oh. Well, I cannot say.

DEBORAH
A perfect gentleman.

TONY
I mean, I do not know.

>   *He flexes his fingers like a safe-cracker.*

TONY
Now perhaps we should remove these visitors before Micheline
awakes.

DEBORAH
You want, like, a spoon?

TONY
I think not. They would find it cold—well, so would she.

DEBORAH
You're going to use your finger?

TONY
I will introduce it, and wait.

He does so.

TONY
Perhaps the wasps will investigate it, and then I can remove both it and them.

DEBORAH
Are you having fun?

TONY
Well: yes. It is good to be useful.

Pause. Deborah moves closer to look.

TONY
They are reluctant to move.

DEBORAH
Nudge 'em.

TONY
I think a gentle touch, with patience, has the best chance.

DEBORAH
Where did she find you?

TONY
I found her here. I do not think she has found me, yet.

DEBORAH
I'm sure that makes sense.

TONY
Ah, here is one. All of a sudden it is starting to move. Gently, gently...

DEBORAH
Is it—?

TONY
Shh.

DEBORAH
Sorry.

>   *Tony slowly withdraws his hand from Micheline's chest. Moves away, looking around.*

DEBORAH
Let it go! Let it go!

TONY
I fear it is interested in the suntan oil on my hands. I should have thought of that.

DEBORAH
Clap your hands!

>   *Tony looks at her.*

DEBORAH
Okay: bad idea.

MICHELINE
(Coming to)
Mmm. Oh, I had such a dream—

DEBORAH
Was there a man in it with his hand down your front?

MICHELINE
What?
She starts to turn; stops. Peers down her front

MICHELINE
What? Oh, my God—you got them out?

TONY
Only one so far. We are about to bestow it on this lovely plant.

MICHELINE
Hurry up, hurry up! This one's getting all excited.

DEBORAH
Blow on it.

MICHELINE
How could I fall asleep? How long was I asleep?

DEBORAH
Just long enough. Tony is wonderful.

TONY
(releasing the wasp into the plant)
There we are. Safely bestowed.

DEBORAH
What hands.

MICHELINE
What do you mean, "what hands"?

DEBORAH
You shouldn't have dozed off.

MICHELINE
I'm awake now, and I want this to be over!
(To the wasp)
Hush, now. Hush, now. Good wasp.

DEBORAH
You're going to have to get rid of it, you know. The landlord doesn't
allow pets.

MICHELINE
I should just...Wasps are the ones that can sting lots of times, right?
Not just once?

DEBORAH
Right.

MICHELINE
Rrrr. Tony. Tony, we aren't done here.

DEBORAH
Now he's nodded off.

TONY
Indeed not. I am refreshing my eyes with this enticing vision.

DEBORAH
What?

TONY
This dress. This gown. This marvelous red shift.

DEBORAH
What, that old thing?

MICHELINE
Hey...

DEBORAH
You'd rather look at that dress than down her front?

MICHELINE
He was looking down my front?

DEBORAH
More than looking, sweetie.

MICHELINE
This is so weird.

TONY
How it moves. It breathes in the least breath of air. It must make its
wearer feel proud and daring.

MICHELINE
It's just a dress.

TONY
It is a flame, a river of heat.

DEBORAH
Do you talk like this at work?

TONY
I have never spoken like this before. I have before my eyes the
image of Micheline dancing, dancing in that dress. It is like nothing
I have ever seen.

DEBORAH
(to Micheline)
You went dancing in that dress?

MICHELINE
Get real.

DEBORAH
(to Tony)
She went dancing with you in that dress?

TONY
Not yet.

> *Deborah starts reeling in the clothesline. There are a couple of towels, and then the dress, followed by other laundry. She puts the pins in a container, and dumps the towels on the deck.*

DEBORAH
So what were you wearing, then? When you met.

MICHELINE
Hey, what about this bug?

DEBORAH
What was she wearing when you met?

TONY
She was wearing a little bathing suit.

DEBORAH
What?

TONY
We are meeting now, Deborah. She is wearing what she is wearing,

and we are meeting now.

DEBORAH
But how—? What about the dress?

MICHELINE
He saw the dress and climbed up here, okay? I am not responsible
for any of this.

DEBORAH
You climbed up here for the dress?

TONY
It is the bravest thing I have ever done, for I did not know how I
would explain myself to Micheline. I still do not know. That dress
calls to my heart, and I must respond.

DEBORAH
You don't even know her?

MICHELINE
If you get rid of this thing for me, I will wear that dress for you,
Tony.

TONY
You will?

MICHELINE
I will. I will put it on and I will stand on a table and I will do the
chicken dance for you, okay? Anything you want. It's buzzing—get
this thing off me before it drills a hole in my chest!

TONY
If it is now awake...

MICHELINE
You want the dance? Do it!

Tony ponders. Then crosses to Micheline.

TONY
All right. For you I would do whatever—

MICHELINE
Just do it!

DEBORAH
But this is *my* dress.

TONY
What?

MICHELINE
Come on, come on.

DEBORAH
This is my dress. This isn't her dress. She never had a dress like this. It wouldn't even fit her.

MICHELINE
Tony, come on.

TONY
(to Deborah)
It is your dress?

MICHELINE
Tony, it's mine, I swear it. Just get rid of this wasp and I'll show you.

TONY
(to Deborah)
It is yours?

Deborah holds it up against her body and sways.

DEBORAH
Fits me in all the right places.

MICHELINE
She's lying. She's making it up. She'll just say anything to impress you. It's my dress.

TONY
(to Micheline)
It is really yours?

DEBORAH
(dancing slowly)
She's a thief, Tony. She's been sucking up my life ever since she moved in here. She can't have this, too.

MICHELINE
Tony, I need your help.

TONY
Yes, of course...but I need to know.

MICHELINE
No, you don't.

TONY
I have climbed too far and risked too much not to know.

MICHELINE
You mean, if it's not my dress, you wouldn't help me? What kind of

a friend is that?

TONY
If it were not your dress, and you said it was...
(puts his hand to his head.)

DEBORAH
Tony, you're not going to say she deserves to be stung!

TONY
No. I don't think so.

MICHELINE
You don't *think* so?
(looking down)
Ahhhhh....

TONY
But I do not deserve to be stung, either.

He slips her straps back up on her shoulders.

MICHELINE
Wait! Wait! You wouldn't do that for me?

DEBORAH
Would you do it for her if she had the dress?

TONY
Uh—

DEBORAH
Would you do it for me if I had that wasp?

TONY
I do not know what to think.

MICHELINE
Don't think: just do it!

TONY
But—

MICHELINE
You promised!

TONY
I did? Perhaps I did...

>	*He starts to reach down.*
>	*Deborah stops dancing.*

DEBORAH
I'm tired of this dress.

>	*Tony stops, watching her.*

DEBORAH
It doesn't make me feel right any more. I don't know where it's been. It may even have been on her.

TONY
But the shift is so beautiful—

MICHELINE
Forget about the dress!

TONY
How can you say that?

MICHELINE
Because things are coming to a crisis down here.

TONY
You don't understand.
(to Deborah)
I believe now it is your dress. Would you dispose of it? Why? It is a miracle of a dress.

DEBORAH
It works too well. I see you looking at me, dressing me with your eyes—it's too scary.

TONY
How can there be too much of a good thing?

He moves toward Deborah. She backs toward the rail.

MICHELINE
Hey—

TONY
I am not proud of it, but that shift makes me giddy and wise at the same time. It makes me more than I was. I will adore her who wears it.

DEBORAH
Nope. I'm done with it.

MICHELINE
Then give it to me! Give it to me!

DEBORAH
It wouldn't fit you.

MICHELINE
I don't care!

TONY
I would.

DEBORAH
Tony, I'll give it to you.

TONY
To me?

DEBORAH
Isn't that what you want?

MICHELINE
No! Give it to me!

DEBORAH
You don't care about her—certainly not about me. Isn't this what you want?

She holds the dress out toward him.

TONY
I want...I want—

MICHELINE
Tony!

DEBORAH
Going...going...

TONY
Yes! Give it to me!

Deborah swivels her arm out over the rail, and drops the dress.

TONY
Ahh!

MICHELINE
What? What?

DEBORAH
It's yours: go get it.

Tony hesitates. Then he strides to Micheline and thwacks her between the breasts. She falls over backwards. Tony rushes to the rail, swings one leg over.

TONY
You just don't understand.

DEBORAH
I hope not.

Tony EXITS hurriedly, climbing down.

DEBORAH
(to Micheline)
Are you all right?

MICHELINE
Ow.

She sits up. Looks into her bra.

DEBORAH
Did it sting you?

MICHELINE
Ow. I can't tell. It's squished all over everywhere. My hero. Eeyew.

DEBORAH
(looking over the rail)
Tony was right, you know. That was a one nice shift.

MICHELINE
I didn't even see his face.
(standing)
My legs are asleep.

DEBORAH
He wasn't your type.

MICHELINE
I am never going to sunbathe again.

DEBORAH
(crossing to her)
Come on. Take a shower and wash it all off.

She starts to help Micheline offstage.

MICHELINE
He had strong hands. Was he cute?

DEBORAH
He dressed well. The clothes made the man.

MICHELINE
I'm sorry about reading your diary.

DEBORAH
Forget it.

MICHELINE
...But don't put this in it, okay?

DEBORAH
Who would believe it?

Blackout

Intermission

Lucked

Part of a baseball diamond. The pitcher's mound and second base are in view. RED, LEROY, and DWAYNE are gathered in conference on the mound. They are looking OL. All have baseball caps and gloves; RED is wearing a warmup jacket.

DWAYNE
So...you think Teddy's gonna be all right?

RED
He'll be fine, Dwayne. Put a little ice on it, he'll be fine. He'll be fine.

LEROY
Red, I never seen Teddy cry before.

RED
Shock. It was just shock.

LEROY
He was crying, Red. The tears were jumping right off of his face.

RED
That's because they were hitting him for distance, and he isn't used to that. That was shame.

LEROY
That was pain. He told you two innings ago his arm was going.

RED
He'd say anything to get off the mound today.

LEROY
That was pain. When his arm went, I heard the 'pop' all the way over to second base.

RED
He's gonna be fine! Some ice, and he'll be fine. Forget about it.

LEROY
I just—

REDForget about it. We got a game to win. We'd of won it already if Teddy wasn't such a—

LEROY
He blew out his arm for you!

RED
Forget about it!

DWAYNE
I think they could hit anybody. They could hit Roger Clemens. Even their outs are hard outs.

RED
Then we'll get hard outs. All we gotta get is just one more.

LEROY
We needed just one more out, four runs ago.

RED
It isn't magic. They're just hitting them where we ain't.

LEROY
Did you see that home run? That was hit. They hit that one where nobody ain't.

RED
You got a brighter idea? You want to maybe quit and go home? Or we could forfeit right now, I guess.

LEROY
I...no, I—

RED
I could announce it right now: Leroy Freeman, who has not missed a game in three years of senior fast-pitch ball, would like to go home and have a nap now, so he quits.

LEROY
I don't quit. I'm just saying.

RED
Just saying what?

LEROY
That...that...what Dwayne said. They could hit anybody, the way they're swinging.

RED
That's why I kept Teddy in. he's the best pitcher.

LEROY
Was.

RED
Is. *Is*. He's gonna be fine. And we're gonna get out of this inning.

DWAYNE
So...who's going to pitch, then? Who could step in for Teddy?
Because I—

RED
Me.

LEROY
You?!

DWAYNE
Because I've been—

RED
(removing his jacket) Me. I'm on the roster: player-manager.

LEROY
You haven't pitched for years.

RED
You have a better idea?

DWAYNE
I could—

LEROY
"Forfeit" is beginning to look good.

> *Red hands his jacket to Dwayne, who stares at it, and then*
> *gives a little gesture of frustration and runs OL with it,*
> *returning almost immediately without it, but with Red's*
> *glove.*

RED
I used to be a starter. I had a tryout with the Dodgers.

LEROY
When they were the Brooklyn Dodgers.

RED
You know too little to talk so much. I'm pitching. Geez, how much worse can it be?
(to the umpire)
I'm pitching: Red Evans. Five warmups.

DWAYNE
There's other guys on the bench. Or I could—

RED
(taking the glove)
Do you see anybody on our bench waving his arm and saying, 'Pick me, Red!'? Do you see them sitting there with towels over their heads, looking very carefully at their hangnails, working on their excuses? If I waved at one of them now, they'd faint.

DWAYNE
(to Leroy)
Why don't they want to try? If you try, there might at least be a miracle. What do they come here for, anyway?

LEROY
They get out of the house, they get to sit in the sun, and there's beer afterwards. Why wouldn't they come?

DWAYNE
I'd pitch, if he asked me.

LEROY
You'd do anything, if he asked you.

DWAYNE
We shouldn't let him pitch.

LEROY
Are you thinking of a mutiny?

DWAYNE
Well, no.

LEROY
Because it's his equipment, and his store is our sponsor, and he buys the beer afterwards. I think if he wants to be the damn umpire, we gotta let him.

Red winds up and throws a pitch.

LEROY
We should all play deep, eh, skipper?

RED
Shut up.

He receives the ball back. Throws again.

DWAYNE
That wasn't bad. That wasn't bad. Nice, floating change-up.

LEROY
That was his fastball. Maybe they just won't believe their eyes.

Red receives the ball.

RED
Listen, you guys: I have played too hard and too smart and too long to get beaten today, or any other day, by a bunch of barnstorming girls. We can't get wiped out by a girls' team. We'll never be able to go into the Legion again.

LEROY
Red. This is not just any girls' team.

DWAYNE
They're really very good. Their record over this tour is 27 wins and only—

LEROY
I never saw guys hit Teddy the way these girls hit him.

    Red throws a pitch.

RED
There: see that? It stops here.

DWAYNE
(to Leroy)
That one wasn't too bad.

LEROY
Red, you don't have to do this. Think with your head. We are now fourteen runs behind and we have got four hits and a walk all day. What is it all about? We are not going to win this game.

RED
It's about this: if they get fifteen runs ahead, they hit the mercy rule and the game is over. Fifteen runs ahead and it's all over. Except it won't be over. From here until the end of baseball, the record will show that the mercy rule was invoked on us. On our team—my team. That the girls didn't just beat us: they didn't even *notice* us.

LEROY
But, Red, we have that rule because blowouts sometimes happen.

RED
But not to us.

LEROY
Look, 14 runs, 15 runs—people are still going to laugh—

RED
You want people to point at you every time you walk out on this
field? You want people to whisper about you when you walk
downtown: "He was on the team that got whipped by a bunch of
little girls"? What will your wife say about that?

LEROY
My wife?

RED
Yeah, the one who's always after you not to slide, you might get
hurt. The one who calls the bar an hour after the game to see if
you're coming home yet. The one who pats your head and calls you
My Little Man.

LEROY
Leave my wife out of this! It's got nothing to do with her. You just
pitch the damn ball, and let's get it over with.

> *He marches to his second-base position.*
> *Red looks at Dwayne.*

DWAYNE
I didn't say nothing.

RED
You going to play or you going to wuss?

DWAYNE
I'm going to play.

He takes his position at first base.

RED
I haven't seen nuthin' so far. Makes me wonder why I let you start.

DWAYNE
You let me start because Jerry's away on his honeymoon.

RED
So who's getting more hits today, Dwayne: Jerry or you?

LEROY
Jerry's scoring all over the place, and he ain't even got his uniform on!

Leroy and Red cackle and guffaw. Dwayne smiles thinly.

RED
(good humour restored)
Gentlemen, gentlemen, please: there are ladies present. All right, then.
(to the umpire)
Ready to go!

UMPIRE [off]
Batter up!

RED
(peering in at the plate)
What do we have here?

LEROY
(running to him) That's the one, Red. That's the one who hit that home run that never came down. She's the gunner.

RED
Oh. Yeah.

DWAYNE
(running to him)
Double, two triples, two loud outs, and the mother of all homers.

RED
(calling to the outfield)
Deep! Play deep. Deeper!...That's good.
(To Leroy) Infield deep, too.

LEROY
(as he and Dwayne go back to their positions)
Like I said before.

RED
Shut up and get your glove on it.

DWAYNE
(loyally) *If* she hits it.

RED
Right. All right, then. Pitch her low.

> *He scowls in toward home plate, shakes off a sign, nods,*
> *winds up, pitches. The fielders crouch in readiness, then relax.*

UMPIRE
(off)
Ball.

LEROY
That's too low.

RED
I know. Play deeper.

> *Leroy moves upstage. Red glares at Dwayne.*

DWAYNE
I didn't say nuthin'.

RED
Deeper.

> *Dwayne takes a step back. Red prepares.*

RED
Okay: low again.

> *He winds up and pitches. The fielders crouch, flinch back, then start forward.*

RED
Bunt?

LEROY & DWAYNE
Bunt!

> *They converge DSC. Red picks up the ball, starts to throw to first, collides with Leroy. Leroy flings himself out of the way, colliding with Dwayne, but by then it is too late.*

RED
I knew it. I just knew it.

DWAYNE
But if you knew it, why did you send us deep?

RED

If I had brought you in, she would have hit it long. I just knew it!

DWAYNE
Look on the bright side, Red. If she's on first, she can't hit it long.

RED
If she had swung for real, she would have whiffed. I had her beat.

LEROY
Boy, that was the perfect bunt, though. Did you see how she laid it down? It just flowed off the bat and rolled—hey!

He has turned toward first base.

LEROY
Steal! She's stealing!

RED
What the—?

He turns to throw to second base—Dwayne and Leroy duck in self-defence—but there is nobody to throw to.
  BECKY arrives from OL and reaches second base without sliding.

RED
Where are you guys? Who's covering second?

LEROY
We came in on the bunt.

DWAYNE
Sorry, Red.

RED
You're supposed to cover second.

LEROY
Sorry, Red.

RED
(to Becky)
What are you doing here? Go back to first—the play was over.

BECKY
Says who?

RED
Everybody knows it was over. You made your cute little bunt, and
we picked it up and chose not to throw you out. End of play.

BECKY
Did you call time?

RED
Well—

BECKY
(to Dwayne)
Did you hear him call time?

DWAYNE
Uh, no.

RED
Any guy would know the play was over.

BECKY
After I hit first base, which way did I turn?

RED
What?

BECKY
Which way did I turn: right into foul territory, or left toward
second base? If I turned right into foul, the play is over. But I
turned left and if you had made your throw and if your first
baseman had caught it he could have tagged me out, if he could
have caught me, and you wouldn't have wanted the play over
before that, would you have?

The men look at each other.

LEROY
(reluctantly)
She turned left, Red.

RED
Oh, hell. Anybody with a brain knows the play was over.

*He turns to appeal to the home plate ump, then looks back at
Becky.*

RED
Time out, okay? You understand now: time out?

BECKY
Yup.

*She ostentatiously steps off second and bends to adjust her
shoes. Her rear is toward Dwayne. He starts nervously and
turns away.*
Red comes DC toward the umpire.

RED
Anybody with a brain would know she's gotta go back. How about
it, ump? She's gotta go back, right? The play was over, right?

The men stare DC. Then Red takes off his hat and flings it on the ground.

LEROY
"Anybody with a brain," he says. And then he asks the ump.

RED
I don't believe it.

He scoops up his hat. To Becky.

RED
Your kind are spoiling our game.

BECKY
With what? The home run? The unassisted double play?

RED
That was luck. Just luck.

BECKY
(back on second base)
Well, then, Red: you and your buddies have been royally *lucked*. We have lucked you out.

Red takes a step toward her.

BECKY
Oh, come and hit me, tough guy. You're 0-for-3 so far today. Hit me: right here
(her chin)
and you will connect with my power attorneys before you reach your dugout.

LEROY
(between them)
Okay, okay.

RED
You half-ripe Barbie doll, I—

LEROY
You get yourself thrown out of here and we will forfeit, and that will be *that*.

> Pause. Then Red moves back to the mound. Leroy moves with him.

LEROY
Now first base is free—

BECKY
Mister Lucky.

LEROY
With first open, you can do what you want with the next batter. This is a good thing, Red.

RED
If that twinkie steals third, will it be an even better thing?

LEROY
She isn't going to steal nothing else.

BECKY
Not me, Red: I promise!

LEROY
Just look at the batter. Focus on the batter. Walk her, or do what you want, but never mind the skirt on second.

RED
I can't walk her. I can't fill up the bases.

LEROY
Sure you can, if you want to. All you have to get is one out. You can do whatever you want. You're the pitcher.

RED
Okay. Okay.

LEROY
(retreating to his position)
Play ball, ump?

UMPIRE
(off)
Batter up!

> *Red settles himself on the mound and peers in for the sign. The other players take their positions, Becky with a short lead off second. Red accepts a sign, then begins to settle himself for the windup. He takes a deep breath.*

BECKY
Just don't pitch her low and in.

RED
(Concentration broken)
What?

BECKY
Just don't pitch her low and in.

RED
(to ump)
Time out! Time out!

(to Becky)
What if I do? Will she not hit it? Or will she hit it big?

BECKY
Just don't do it.

LEROY
Shut up, runner. Come on, Red.

RED
Where did Teddy pitch her?

DWAYNE
Down and in twice. Up and in once. Up and out once. She got a hit each time.

BECKY
Pitch her right down the middle. She won't be looking for that.

RED
How about I park my rosin bag in your mouth? She wouldn't expect that, either.

BECKY
Your rosin bag is so small, I wouldn't even notice it.

     She laughs at her own joke; slaps her knee.

UMPIRE
(off)
We here to play or we here to talk?

RED
Play—we're here to play.

UMPIRE
(off)
Batter up!

Red addresses home plate, shakes off the sign. Becky shakes it off with him. Red gets a sign he likes, winds up, delivers. All poise for the play, then relax. Becky returns to second base.

UMPIRE
(off)
Ball!

LEROY
That's where you wanted it, Red? Out and down?

RED
(receiving ball)
Yeah. Sure. Why?

DWAYNE
The book on her says she loves to hit out and down.

RED
Oh. So what doesn't she hit?

BECKY
Small children in crosswalks.

    The men stare at her.

BECKY
Not a word.

    She mimes zipping her lip.

LEROY
All you can do, Red, is pitch her honest. I'm sorry, but that's the only thing left. Just pitch her honest, and if she hits it, we'll just have to catch it for you.

RED
"Pitch her honest"—what is that? Just throw the ball, without any kind of plan? What sort of baseball is that? I'll throw it through her ear before I'll "pitch her honest". You gotta have a plan: pitch her outside and outside and then way deep in when she's reaching for the next outside pitch. Or...outside again, because you know she'll be waiting for the inside deep one. You gotta think. "Honest" won't get you anywhere all by itself. You got to give the game a nudge.

UMPIRE
(off)
Hey!

RED
Just a minute: mound conference!
(to Leroy)
But it's gotta be the right nudge. Not like Teddy and the hair cream: you remember when he was going to use a grease ball and he had that little bottle of hair cream in his pocket and he got some on the ball and he went to pitch and—whup—that sucker was so slippery he threw it behind him on the windup all the way to the center fielder. That was too much nudge. And my problem here, I can't see what nudge to put, or where to put it.

LEROY
Can't help you there, Red.

RED
I know.
(to the ump)
Okay.

UMPIRE
(off)
Batter up!

RED
All right, then.

     He takes a breath. Then turns to Leroy.

RED
Hey—how about a little chatter? This infield sounds like a library reading room.

LEROY
I can only chatter when we're ahead.

DWAYNE
Um.

BECKY
Hum-baby, hum-baby, lay it in there, lay it in there. Red, Red, he's our man: if he can't do it, no one can. Put it in there. Put it in there. Give to her good, Red. If she says no, you know that's gotta mean yes. Put it right through here. Hole in the bat, hole in the bat. Hum-baby, hum-baby. Yo-batter-batter-batter. Yo-batter-batter-batter. Pitcher-pitcher-pitcher-pitcher-pitcher-pitcher-pitcher: hey!...You mean chatter like that? Or would you prefer it to rhyme throughout?

RED
Go to third.

BECKY
What?

RED
Go to third. Go on: take the base. Just shut up and do it.

BECKY
(to Dwayne)
I bet he says that to all the girls.

RED
I won't throw. I give you my word.

BECKY
Your word? Red, your word is a turd.

RED
You have no respect for the traditions of baseball, and I want you off my infield. Take third base!

BECKY
No respect? I've had more good innings than you've had hot suppers. I love baseball. I don't just cling to it, with my belly hanging down, because I can't think of anything else to do with my weekends.

Baseball is sweet and funny and the perfect balance of attack and defence. Think of the infield out, the wimpiest thing you can do: the batter runs, the infielder runs, the infielder throws, the first-baseman stretches, the runner lunges—just a wimpy little out, but he's only out by maybe a step, maybe two. It's so close, so balanced...I can play all afternoon, and lose 1-0, and know what I was playing was good.

Red, as far as I can see, for you it's only baseball if you win. If you don't win, you wuz robbed, you wuz let down, the ump was blind, the wind was wrong, the bat was corked, the ball was dead, the crowd was hostile, or Mars was misaligned with Saturn in conjunction with Uranus. Uranus the planet.

RED
I—

BECKY
After all these years of playing, Red, you should have figured it out: half the time you lose. That's the way it is. The worst team in the league can beat the best team once in a while—and you never know when you go into a game whether this is that once-in-a-while. That's why we keep coming back to play. That's why the fans keep coming back to watch.

So pull out your thumb, chum, and pitch—win or lose. For the love of baseball. If we win, you buy me a beer later. If you win, I'll buy you a case.

Whew: now I can't steal third: I'm all out of breath.

Red is at a loss.

BECKY
At a loss? Pitch: don't talk.

After a moment, Red turns toward home. He sizes up the batter. Becky takes her lead.

DWAYNE
Time out! Time out!

He runs to the mound.

BECKY
You hoping the sun will set?

RED
Now what?

DWAYNE
I got an idea.

RED
Just what we need.

DWAYNE
No, really: it might help.

RED
What, then? What? What?

DWAYNE
It's just this: she's had four at-bats, not counting the walk and when Teddy hit her.

LEROY
(joining them)
Four-for-four. No matter what he pitched her.

DWAYNE
And—no matter what he pitched her, she hit a ground ball single up the right side.

LEROY
She did?

DWAYNE
She did. They were screamers, but they were all through the same place.

LEROY
I think he's right.

RED
And you missed every one.

LEROY
I'm not fourteen feet wide. And she hits it where I ain't. Every time.

Becky sits on second base.

DWAYNE
Another single will score that little scooter from second. And that will be the ball game.

RED
So...?

DWAYNE
So you got to walk her.

RED
No.

BECKY
We want action, we want action, we want action—

DWAYNE
You got to. And face whoever comes next.

RED
Hey, runner: you know your baseball, huh?

BECKY
Yup. And this ain't it.

RED
You ever hear of "The Boudreau Shift"?

BECKY
Of course. Lou Boudreau shifted the infield way over to try to stop Ted Williams, who always hit to right field. Why?

RED
You are about to see "The Red Shift".

LEROY and DWAYNE
"The Red Shift"?

RED
"The Red Shift." Dwayne—
(gesturing L)
get over here. Stand partway between the mound and first base.
Leroy, play between Dwayne and first. When she hits it, just stick
your glove out and you've got her. Last out. Just don't catch the tip
of her bat as she swings—that would be interference.

DWAYNE
Way in here? Why can't I play deeper? Like Boudreau did.

RED
'Cause Ted Williams kept on getting hits.

DWAYNE
But this is too close.

RED
And I don't want another bunt to mess us up. I don't know why I
didn't think of this before.
(to outfield)
Play over! Way over! And shallow! That's it.

LEROY
This is suicide.

RED
You going to take your position, or not?

LEROY
I love my teeth more than I love you, Red. I'll play where I always play.

RED
You do that, you'll never play for me again.

BECKY
"The Red Shift." That's not such a bad idea, Red. It may work. If Nancy doesn't punch it to left.

RED
She won't. I don't even think she can. If she tries, I'll strike her out.

BECKY
You should bring your third baseman over, too.

RED
When I want your advice, I'll ask for it.
(calling to third base)
Bob, move a little toward shortstop....Okay, but watch for the steal.

DWAYNE
This is awful close.

RED
Just knock the ball down, Dwayne. If you can't catch it clean, knock it down. We'll have plenty of time to throw her out.

BECKY
Red, if this works, it will make your name.

DWAYNE
The Red Shift.

BECKY
Of course, you'll have to change your last name to 'Shift'.

RED
(to the umpire)
All right.

UMPIRE
(off)
Batter up!

DWAYNE
(as the players prepare)
You know, Red, I used to be content when I just sat on the bench, and only got in the game in the late innings, when we were so far ahead or so far behind that it didn't matter much. And then I used to be content to pinch-hit, pinch-run...whatever you wanted.

And then I was content to be your tenth man, ready for any position if somebody didn't show up. And then I was content just to bat at the tail of the lineup and play right field, even when nobody on the other team could hit to right.

How many years have we been playing senior ball, Red Saturday mornings, Sunday afternoons, until our own kids don't recognize us unless we're wearing shirts with numbers on them.

I love baseball. And I'll even stand here and do this for you. I'll stand here, where I can feel the batter's breath, where that fat-barreled bat is so close I could kiss it, and I will try to catch what she hits.

But I got to tell you now, while I still can, Red, that I don't feel content any more.

> *Red, who has gradually climbed down from his windup, stares at him, and then at Leroy.*

LEROY
I didn't say nothing.

BECKY
I didn't say nothing.

DWAYNE
Is the whole game really only about what the guy wants who owns
the ball, Red? Is it really only about who owns the team?

RED
It's about getting one more out.

DWAYNE
What I like about baseball is that there isn't any clock. It isn't like
basketball with its ten-second rules and the time running down,
running down. This inning here could go on forever, except for the
mercy rule.
　　Why have the mercy rule, Red? You don't even believe in mercy.
Let them go on getting hits. Let us go on trying to stop them—let
the inning go on forever.

RED
I want it over, and I want it over now. I want to show them, once
and for all. Stick out your glove, Dwayne; stick out that golden
glove. You're gonna become immortal.

LEROY
"The Dwayne Shift"? I don't think so.

RED
He's gonna be immortal! So let's do it.

UMPIRE
(off)
Batter up!

DWAYNE
(As everybody prepares)
So...you think Teddy's gonna be all right?

> *Players crouch. Red pitches. Becky starts to run toward third. Dwayne brings his hands up toward his stomach as if trying to catch a line drive.*

> *Freeze.*

> *Blackout.*

Swift-Tuttle

The relationships in this play:
UNCLE OTTO, a retired scientist
MARCUS, his nephew-in-law twice over
CHLOE, niece to Otto, wife to Marcus
DAPHNE, her sister; niece to Otto, exÄwife to Marcus
MIKE, Daphne's boyfriend

A field, long past midnight in early August.

MARCUS
(off)
Here?

OTTO
(off)
A little further, I think.

MARCUS
(off)
This chair—oof—was not designed for—oof—off-road use, Uncle
Otto.

OTTO
(off: laughing)
No, of course not. Onward!

MARCUS
(off)
Oof.

> OTTO ENTERS, seated in a wheelchair which MARCUS is
> pushing. Otto has a tartan rug over his knees, a white hat,
> and a scarf around his neck over his white suit. He has a
> thermos of coffee.
>   Marcus is dressed for the cottage—chinos, sweatshirt,
> shapeless hat.

MARCUS
How much further?

OTTO
Very soon now.

> Wheelchair hits a rut.

OTTO
Careful!

MARCUS
Sorry. It's a little tough navigating when there's no moon.

OTTO
The stars will light your way, Marcus. Onward!

> Wheelchair progresses another few feet.

OTTO
Here: stop. Stop!

MARCUS
Thank God.
He straightens up, rubs his hands.

OTTO
Thank God, indeed, Marcus. Thank him for all the glories of this creation. For stars and their wheeling dance, for the weather front that has given us this clear night, for your youthful vigour that has propelled us here.

MARCUS
Thank God you've lost weight since last year.

OTTO
I come back to this field each August, Marcus.

MARCUS
I know, Uncle Otto.

OTTO
On the clearest night I can get between the 9th and the 12th.

MARCUS
I know.

OTTO
Couldn't get much clearer than this, could you? There is the exaltation of new wine in the air. And it was on just such a night, so long ago—

OTTO and MARCUS
–that I first began to understand.

OTTO
Here I began the voyage of comprehension that took me much,

much further than any lad in a midnight field could hope to go—
awards, honours, publications.

MARCUS
And look where it's got you.

OTTO
Eh? Oh, I see: back in the field after midnight.

> *He laughs ruefully.*

OTTO
My grandfather brought me out that night on his shoulder, and
against my will. I was sleepy, and could not imagine anything
worth stirring for. Now, his father had brought him out to look at
the August sky at a time when people, wise people, thought that
shooting stars were but an atmospheric event, like a rainbow or
fog. But someone had started to look at and to study them, to plow
through the records of past Augusts.

So his father brought my grandfather out to look, and he
brought me out to look. And, having looked, we began to think.

And now I am wheeled out, like a holy statue on a day of
veneration, by my nephew-in-law twice over, when I desire to see
the sky. I see a sort of progress there—do you not?

MARCUS
All I see is a struggle through the dark, with ruts below and biting
insects above, and a tomorrow all out of balance because of too
little sleep tonight.

OTTO
But still you exert yourself, for the honor of the occasion.

MARCUS
I exert myself as your nephew-in-law twice over. If I refused to
push you out here, either Chloe, my wife and your niece, or

Daphne, my ex-wife and your niece, would never let me hear the end of it.

OTTO
And I might cut you out of my will.

MARCUS
Really. The thought that you might do that never crossed my mind.

Lights a match for his cigarette.

OTTO
(Shielding his eyes)
Stop that! Put that out! You know better than that! Put that out!

MARCUS
(putting it out)
It's out, it's out.

OTTO
The eyes must get used to the dark to see the light within it. You know better.

MARCUS
Sorry.

OTTO
It would be bad enough were you to dazzle just your own eyes.

MARCUS
I am terribly sorry, Uncle Otto. I will probably never smoke again, even at high noon in midsummer, because of the grief and chagrin I feel. My heart is filled with the sort of backward-looking, if-only-things-had-been-otherwise nostalgia that is experienced by the characters in significant European movies.
   Ah, me. Now, could we drop it, please?

OTTO
All right. I'm sure it will not matter to me, since it does not matter to you.

>   *Picks at the blanket.*

OTTO
Where are the others?

MARCUS
Still dazzling each other, no doubt. They'll be along soon enough. You promised to explain the Red Shift to Daphne's boyfriend.

OTTO
I did? Who is he?

MARCUS
You did. He's Daphne's merchant banker. He sat beside you at supper.

OTTO
I said I would explain the Red Shift to him? Why would I do that? And tonight, of all nights.

MARCUS
Because you know and he does not. Because he was reading that *Time* magazine cover you have framed in the hall, the one with your face and a banner headline:
(gesturing)
"Fixing The Red Shift"—

OTTO
The girls gave me that. Years ago.

MARCUS
And he said, "What's that about, communism or paint?" And you

said you'd explain it to him.

OTTO
I wish I'd promised something else. The Red Shift...the Red Shift...it's so obvious I can't say it any more.

MARCUS
He'll be disappointed. And Daphne's in one of those moods.
(cheerfully)
No joy for Mike on any front tonight.

OTTO
(grimly)
I'll give him cause for joy. Which way is east?

MARCUS
I'll tell you at sunrise.

OTTO
(pointing out over the audience
That way, I think.

Marcus turns him to face east.

OTTO
Thank you: just so. And a glorious night for viewing. The stars are so near you could pluck them like ...like...

MARCUS
Guitar strings?

OTTO
No...Pluck them like...

MARCUS
Chickens?

OTTO
No!

MARCUS
Eyebrows?

OTTO
Berries! Pluck them like berries!

MARCUS
(considering the sky)
They are?

OTTO
They are. Just beyond an outstretched mind.

> *Beat.*

MARCUS
Should I be watching yet?

OTTO
You should always be watching.

MARCUS
Oh. Right.

> *He slaps at a mosquito.*

MARCUS
You are going to read us this will of yours sometime, Uncle Otto?
For the pleasure of seeing our reactions?

OTTO
Observation is the scientist's chief joy.

MARCUS
If you leave me anything, the only one more outraged than Chloe
will be Daphne.

OTTO
I will keep that in mind.

MARCUS
They would tear me to pieces.

OTTO
But you have already had so much of them, Marcus. Far more than
your share.

MARCUS
Lucky me.

      He feels the ground with his hand, then sits.

OTTO
You have enjoyed marriage with both my nieces.

MARCUS
Can you use "enjoyed" and "marriage" in the same sentence?

OTTO
I have never understood...

MARCUS
Why I married Chloe, having once married Daphne?

OTTO
Were you seeking a rhyme?

MARCUS
For the pleasure of your company, uncle. I would do anything to

stay part of your family.

OTTO
Thank God I have no nephews, then.

CHLOE
(off)
No, this way.

DAPHNE
(off)
This way! That way goes right through the pricker bushes.

CHLOE
(off)
So what? We've got long pants on.

DAPHNE
(off)
But Mike doesn't. He has those gorgeous bare legs.

CHLOE
(off) He'll know to dress right, this time next year. Come on!

MIKE
(off)
Ow! I'm not a wishbone. I can't go both ways at once.

DAPHNE
(off)
Puritan.

MIKE
(off)
Ow!

CHLOE
(off)
Darling Daphne, that is a tree. Your boyfriend cannot go over it, and he is grinding his nose on the bark. One of us will have to let go.

DAPHNE
(off)
He's my guy: you let go.

CHLOE
(off)
But you take such bad care of him. You let him walk into trees.

MIKE
(off)
How about you both let go?

MARCUS
Not in this family. Not in a million years.

DAPHNE
(off)
Poor Mikey. Where does it hurt?

MIKE
(off)
Well, actually, it—

CHLOE
(off)
Does it hurt here?
MIKE
(off)
Hey! Stop—stop!

DAPHNE
(off)
Or here?

MIKE
(off)
Not there!

> *MIKE staggers onstage with CHLOE and DAPHNE, who are each holding one of his hands and tickling him. The women are in comfortable, cozy, flashy clothing. Daphne wears a baseball cap with the brim turned backwards. Mike is dressed for cocktails on a deck: madras shorts, light jacket, open shirt.*

MARCUS
Ladies, ladies.

DAPHNE
Chloe, you can't tickle him there—he's my boyfriend.

CHLOE
I can tickle when I want, whom I want, where I want.

> *She threatens to tickle Mike, who flinches.*

DAPHNE
You think so?

> *She tickles Chloe, who immediately doubles up on the ground to protect herself, and lands on top of her. Mike is left standing as if stranded, gazing blankly about him.*

CHLOE
No no no no no.

DAPHNE
You think—just because you're older—

CHLOE
Stop stop stop.

MIKE
What's going on?

DAPHNE
Just because you're prettier—

CHLOE
I'm not, I'm not, okay? I'm ugly ugly ugly.

MARCUS
(Standing)
She's going to pee herself.

OTTO
Children, children.

DAPHNE
So, who can you tickle?

CHLOE
Nobody, nobody: I can't tickle nobody.

OTTO
Michael, come here would you?

    Mike gropes his way toward the wheelchair.
DAPHNE
That's right.

MARCUS
(lifting Daphne by the arms)
All right, all right—that's enough.

CHLOE
I can only tickle you!

> *She attacks Daphne, who is temporarily helpless.*

DAPHNE
Stop, stop: no fair!

> *She overbalances Marcus, and the three of them collapse in a heap.*

CHLOE
Revenge!

DAPHNE
Oh no, oh no. Let go, you idiot!

MARCUS
Enough, enough!

OTTO
Just here, Michael, a little bit to the right. Good. Here:
(handing him a whistle)
just blow on this, would you?

MIKE
All right...

> *He blows a piercing blast on the whistle. The three on the ground subside. He puts a hand to one ear.*

MIKE
Ow.

DAPHNE
Thank you, darling man. You have saved me from death by joy.

MIKE
Goes right through your head, doesn't it?

Chloe and Daphne help each other to their feet.

OTTO
If you don't care to give the occasion the attention it deserves, you can go in and go to bed.

MARCUS
(flat on the ground)
Can't got to bed now. It's past one in the morning: we'd wake up the whole household.

CHLOE
We are the whole household.

DAPHNE
The nursing staff, darling: how sweet to think of them, Marcus.

MARCUS
(sitting up)
Uncle Otto, we are here. We will strive to be attentive.

OTTO
Good. The meteorites are best viewed by one who is calm, is as still as the night air.

Daphne and Chloe poke at each other then subside.

OTTO
Otherwise, you are always glancing this way and that way, trying to see everything and seeing nothing. It is not work for a jittery spirit.

CHLOE
We know that, Uncle. We were just shaking out all the jitters.

She gyrates for a second, then subsides.

CHLOE
See? All gone.

DAPHNE
(to Marcus, as she helps him up)
And you: watch where you put your hands, Mister Ex-husband.

MARCUS
What are you talking about, Daphne? I was entirely the gentleman.

DAPHNE
Exactly what I mean. How could you miss an opportunity like that? It may not come again.

MARCUS
It always comes again.

DAPHNE
In the future, keep your hands to myself.

MARCUS
And your boyfriend? And your sister, my wife?

DAPHNE
Just how many hands do you have?

She crosses to Chloe.

DAPHNE
Chloe, darling, you have leaves on your butt.

CHLOE
So did Eve.
(brushing at her clothes)
As a fashion statement, it goes a long way back.

DAPHNE
(crossing to Mike.)
Give the nice uncle back his whistle, Mike.

MIKE
Gladly. Where is he?

DAPHNE
Seek the gleam of the Milky Way reflecting in the tubing of his chair.
(turning him toward Otto)
Still nothing?

MIKE
It's a waste of time, Daph. I don't even drive at night.

Daphne takes the whistle and gives it to Otto.

DAPHNE
Nonsense. You just aren't trying hard enough. Make your eyes get used to the darkness. Make an effort to relax.

She goes in search of a soft patch of ground.

MIKE
(still talking at where she was)
Okay: I'll relax if it kills me.

OTTO
How long have you had this condition?

MIKE
I didn't even know it was a condition until I met your niece.

DAPHNE
Chloe, did we bring the blankets?

CHLOE
I'll get them.

> *She retrieves blankets from the pack on the back of the wheelchair. She and Daphne spread a blanket UR of the wheelchair.*

OTTO
You cannot see the stars at all?

MIKE
I've seen photographs of them. When you consider the distances, I probably see them better in a book than you ever do out here.

OTTO
It is not the same thing. Not the same thing at all.

CHLOE
If we put the blanket here, this little rise will sort of prop up our heads, like last year.

DAPHNE
(sitting)
Oh, yes. These are last year's lumps.

MARCUS
(looking up)
Oh, hey! There's one.

DAPHNE
Where?

CHLOE
It's gone now, slowpoke. Its always gone by the time you say,
"Where?", and the other person points, and you look. That's the
one thing I hate about shower nights.

MARCUS
Nice red one.

DAPHNE
Where do we look? I always forget.

OTTO
Out of Perseus. They always come from the direction of the
constellation Perseus. From there.

He points the direction, out over the audience, then smiles.

OTTO
Ah!

MIKE
What?

CHLOE
(sitting)
Oh, that was nice.

OTTO
Very nice.

MARCUS
Mmm.

DAPHNE
I always stare too hard. My eyes get all dry and my neck gets all stiff, and then all of a sudden I wake up and it's hours later and there's a bug walking on my lip.

MARCUS
Lucky bug.

MIKE
That's enough.

DAPHNE
He's just complimenting my lip.

MIKE
With all respect, Marcus, she is not your wife anymore. I'll thank you not to compliment her lip.

MARCUS
With all respect, Michael, would you prefer me to insult her lip?

MIKE
I would prefer you to leave her lip alone.

DAPHNE and CHLOE
Fight-fight-fight-fight.

MARCUS
You can stop me. If you can find me.

DAPHNE and CHLOE
(of the men)
Oooh.

(and then, at the sky)
Oooh!

OTTO
That was a skipper.

DAPHNE
I saw that one! I saw that one!

CHLOE
It was just like a dotted line.

OTTO
It grazed the outer atmosphere like flat stone kissing the surface of a pond—skip, skip, skip—and it is on its way again. We may meet that very rock again many Augusts from now.

DAPHNE
I never see the good ones. Do I get a prize?

OTTO
The seeing is the prize, Daphne.

DAPHNE
Oh.

CHLOE
You get one free wish. Courtesy of me.

DAPHNE
Yippee!

CHLOE
But you have to use it tonight.

DAPHNE
(pondering)
A free wish, a free wish, a free wish...

MIKE
So, Dr. Schiller—

OTTO
"Uncle Otto", please.

MIKE
So, Uncle Otto. These meteors are coming from the constellation Perseus?

DAPHNE
Yes.

OTTO
No.

MIKE
Well, that clears it up.

OTTO
They come from the radiant, the *direction* of Perseus, Michael. That's where we look in the sky. But they are part of our solar system, debris of a comet in orbit around our sun. When we run through the debris stream each year, we meet it in such a way that, if we look toward Perseus on its rising, we see little bits of comet burning up in our atmosphere—like that.

MIKE
Like what?

CHLOE
Two at once.

DAPHNE
I saw that one, too. Do I get another wish?

CHLOE
One per customer.

MIKE
I don't understand.

MARCUS
Walk down to the end of the field: you can see them better if you're closer to them.

MIKE
This happens every year? They don't run out?

OTTO
They are very many, and very small, and there are more every time their comet mother makes her orbit. She last came by in 1992, and that was a noble summer for shooting stars.

MIKE
And the comet comes back—?

OTTO
Every 130 years.

MARCUS
Book your tickets now.

MIKE
And the little rocks that fall off the comet just drift around?

OTTO
Oh, no: they are in orbit, too. We are all in orbit. The earth and the planets and the comet and its debris around the sun; the whole

system around the centre of our galaxy; the whole galaxy in orbit around what seems to us now to be the centre of the universe; and perhaps that, too, in orbit around some great thing we cannot yet comprehend.

MIKE
But—

> *Otto claps his hands once.*

OTTO
A demonstration, then. A model, to help you appreciate the reality.

MIKE
Please don't bother—

OTTO
You have come all the way into this field: it's the least we can do. Now: I will be the sun.

MARCUS
Around you we all revolve.

OTTO
And you, Michael, will be the earth, secure in your orbit. Daphne will be your moon, and she can guide you over the rough bits.

DAPHNE
Oh, Mikey, I get to moon you! I told you this would be a fun night.

> *She grabs his arm.*

MIKE
Stop it.

DAPHNE
Baby, when I am a glowing full moon, I have to revolve around and around on you.

MIKE
Stop it. This is embarrassing.

DAPHNE
Don't be such a poop.

MIKE
You just go too far all the time.

DAPHNE
I can't, my sweet, because I orbit you as surely as you orbit the sun. Come on, now: sooner started, sooner over.

> *She tugs him by the arm, and they start to make a circle around Otto.*

DAPHNE
Your gravity has always attracted me.

MIKE
But what's the point? I can't see a damned thing.

OTTO
But you can hear. So you can tell from my voice where I am. And around me you orbit, one circuit per year. This is not to scale, you realize.

MIKE
Thank you.

OTTO
Good. And all the other planets orbit as well, each in her own track,

never colliding. But there are also other heavenly bodies, and the orbits of some of them intersect with the orbit of earth.

CHLOE
I'm the heavenly body, right? Right.

OTTO
Your full name is "109P Swift/Tuttle", and your cometary orbit is a deep oval that swings close to the sun every 130 years.

CHLOE
Here I go: woosh!

> *Her orbit may carry her offstage, or down among the audience, depending on the playing space.*

CHLOE
Swift-Tuttle, Swift-Tuttle, Swift-Tuttle, Swift-Tuttle. I'm slowing down. Swift...Tuttle, Swift...Tuttle.

MIKE
Is this the Red Shift part?

OTTO
No. Hardly to do with it at all. The Red Shift—

CHLOE
Now I'm making my turn back toward the sun. Swift...Tuttle. Swift, Tuttle. Swift-Tuttle, Swift-Tuttle.

> *She races back toward OTTO, circles him, and races away again running backwards.*

CHLOE
You can tell I'm a comet because I have a tail, and my tail is always facing away from the sun.

OTTO
Oh, very good!

CHLOE
Swift-Tuttle, Swift-Tuttle, Swift-Tuttle.

DAPHNE
(to Mike)
She missed us this time. But she'll be back.

MIKE
Have you done this before?

DAPHNE
Uncle Otto always has us us demonstrate stuff until he's sure we
get it. One time there was a big house party and he made us do
DNA, and I ended up replicating with Jarvis Jones.

MIKE
You replicated with Jarvis Jones?

DAPHNE
It was all in the name of science.

CHLOE
Swift-Tuttle, Swift-Tuttle. This is much more fun than being a
boring planet stuck in a round orbit. Swift-Tuttle.

OTTO
But she is in her own orbit, Michael, as predictable and regular as
your own.

CHLOE
No way!

OTTO
And as she travels it, she leaves debris: tiny chips of stone and metals.

> *Marcus takes the thermos. and pours a cupful of the contents.*

MARCUS
I'm debris.

DAPHNE
Do tell.

OTTO
A cloud of particles renewed each time the comet makes her orbit. And at one point the orbit of the comet crosses the orbit of earth.

CHLOE
Mike, you naughty boy, your orbit runs right through mine.Here I come: Swift-Tuttle, Swift-Tuttle.

MIKE
I'm tired of this game.

DAPHNE
(touching his forehead)
We're getting some global warming here, Uncle Otto.

OTTO
A moment more.

CHLOE
Swift-Tuttle, Swift-Tuttle: whoo-hoo!

> *She passes close in front of Mike and Daphne, a little away from Otto, and continues her orbit. Marcus takes position where near Mike.*

OTTO
The debris is very small—

MARCUS
Size matters less than how you use it.

OTTO
Exactly. The particles are small, but moving so quickly relative to the earth, that when they hit earth's atmosphere, every August, they light up the night sky.

DAPHNE
Which can't hurt the earth.

OTTO
Not in the least. Like this:

> *Marcus dashes the cup of liquid into Mike's face as Daphne dodges to one side.*

MIKE
What the hell?

MARCUS
It can't harm you, Mike. It's just debris from the comet's tail.

MIKE
Harm me? I'll show you harm, you sonofabitch! Where are you?

MARCUS
Oops—you're in the comet's path again.

> *Another cup full in the face. Then he skips away R.*

MIKE
Arrgh! Come here!

MARCUS
Now, now, you can't leave your orbit.

MIKE
You coward...What a stupid joke.

OTTO
A harmless one, Michael. You will continue. As does the earth.

MIKE
It's not the same thing.

OTTO
It was not to scale—

MIKE
Planets don't have feelings! Little balls of rock don't play stupid tricks. Can't you tell the difference?

OTTO
I can.

MIKE
Do you understand that I cannot see in the dark?

OTTO
Yes.

MIKE
That being in the dark in a strange place, not being able to see a foot in front of you, is frightening?

OTTO
Oh, yes.

MIKE
That it takes the cleverness of a, a tree stump to play a trick on a
blind man in the dark?

MARCUS
(As Chloe joins him)
Who are you calling a tree stump?

MIKE
You let my girlfriend's ex-husband torment me. Why do you do
that?

DAPHNE
Oh, Mikey, don't get all upset.

   She takes his arm; he shakes her off.

MIKE
Daphne, shut up. You make me look like a fool over and over again,
and then you tell me what Marcus would have done. He's not your
husband any more. I don't want to hear about him.

DAPHNE
He's part of the family: you get no choice.

MIKE
I get a choice. I can leave.

DAPHNE
Good: go, leave. Well?

MIKE
What's the project of the night? To make me look foolish?

DAPHNE
(taking his hand)
Come on, Mike—

MIKE
(shaking her off)
Stop pushing me around.

DAPHNE
I'm just trying to—

MIKE
You're trying to push me around. Make me go where you want to go. Do you ever ask where I want to go?

DAPHNE
You don't want to go anywhere!

MIKE
Maybe I'm happy where I am.
(slaps a mosquito)

DAPHNE
Liar.

MIKE
You owe me an apology.

CHLOE and MARCUS
Oh-oh.

DAPHNE
A what?

OTTO
Michael: do not desire the impossible.

MIKE
An apology.

DAPHNE
I never apologize.

MIKE
You are treating me shamefully, and I want no more of it.

DAPHNE
You love it when I treat you shamefully.

MARCUS
I always did.

Chloe gives him an elbow in the ribs.

MIKE
I am not a fool, and I will not be treated like one.

DAPHNE
You are so stupid and stiff! I don't know what I see in you.

CHLOE
(to Marcus)
His money, his car...

He pokes her.

DAPHNE
Who do you think you are to stand in my field and tell me how to behave?

MIKE
It's not your field. It's your uncle's field. You don't have it. You don't have anything except a dangerous bravado which looks really

charming at a cocktail party, but which is growing really, really old on me.

CHLOE and MARCUS
Fight-fight-fight.

DAPHNE and MIKE
Shut up!

OTTO
(looking at the sky)
Oh! That was almost green.

DAPHNE
You—you snail.

MIKE
Daphne, I am very fond of you. But this abuse has to stop. And it has to stop tonight. I want an apology, or the ring goes back to the jeweller.

DAPHNE and CHLOE
The ring?

MARCUS and OTTO
The ring?

DAPHNE
What on earth ring is that?

MIKE
(holding it up)
This one, actually. Of course you could see it better if—

OTTO
No lights! No lights!

MIKE
Okay! Okay!

DAPHNE
That's an engagement ring?

MIKE
Supposed to be.

CHLOE and MARCUS
Ooh.

CHLOE
For me? That amazing thing we looked at last week?

MIKE
Yes, darling.

CHLOE
(moving toward him)
Mikey, you really shouldn't have—

MIKE
And I won't. Unless you apologize.

CHLOE and MARCUS
Ooh.

DAPHNE
What?

MIKE
We are going to start out this marriage right.

DAPHNE
I-don't-apologize.

Mike opens his hand and lets the ring fall.

MIKE
There it is. While you're down there groveling, you can search for it.

> *Chloe and Marcus retreat a step. Daphne steps toward Mike as if to pound him.*

OTTO
Daphne.

> *She stops.*

OTTO
That would not be appropriate.

DAPHNE
(to Mike)
You are not worth an apology.

> *She crosses to Chloe. Mike speaks to where she was.*

MIKE
Fine. Now we'll see if you are.

DAPHNE
(to Chloe)
Did you hear that?

CHLOE
Yes.

DAPHNE
He said—

CHLOE
I know.

DAPHNE
He wants me to—

CHLOE
I know.

DAPHNE
In front of my family.

CHLOE
Men are pigs.

Daphne throws down her hat in frustration.

DAPHNE
Oh! And I thought I had found a good one.

CHLOE
Good pig.

MIKE
(to Otto)
Did you see that?

OTTO
What part of the sky?

MIKE
It's—never mind.

CHLOE
An apology is out of the question.

DAPHNE
I'd rather cut my throat.

> *Beat.*

CHLOE
That was some ring. What I saw of it.

DAPHNE
Oh—what have I done? What have I done?

CHLOE
An apology is out of the question?

> *Mike slaps at a mosquito on his leg. Wipes it off on his sock.*

DAPHNE
Yes. No. Ohh—rats.

> *She stomps UR, flops down on the ground.*

MARCUS
So. An apology was out of the question?

CHLOE
By her, anyhow.

MARCUS
You can't be hoping for an apology from *him.*

CHLOE
There is too much moral high ground around here.

OTTO
(pointing to the sky)
There—there!

MIKE
(looking OL)
Very nice. What time is it?

OTTO
Not much before two. Plenty of good viewing ahead.

MIKE
And when is the Red Shift part?

OTTO
Young man, the Red Shift has nothing at all to do with what we are seeing. The meteorites glow because of friction with our atmosphere: heat, friction. They burn, they shine. We see the Red Shift in the light from stars, far beyond them, bending to gravity, stretching as they fly from us or toward us. It is the wondrous trail of the dance of the stars, and once I knew it well. But you cannot study it here, in this field.

MIKE
But I thought—

OTTO
You were mistaken.

MIKE
Great.

OTTO
Don't be cast down. You came to find one thing, and you are finding many others. The Red Shift will always be there another time.

CHLOE
He's frightened, that's all. Out of his element. In the dark.

MARCUS
Someone should comfort your sister.

CHLOE
He should.

MARCUS
Someone should.

CHLOE
They're a pretty good match in daylight.

MARCUS
He's a cranky old lady.

CHLOE
But he has that great body.

MARCUS
So. His end justifies his mien?

CHLOE
Do you think they'll make up? We're got four more days here. I can't take four days of this.

MARCUS
We could leave.

CHLOE
Uncle Otto...

MARCUS
Oh, yes. What would he think of your abandoning him?

Chloe elbows him.

OTTO
(gazing at the sky]
Ah! A bright one, yes.

MIKE
Lovely.

CHLOE
(picking up Daphne's hat)
You should comfort your sister-in-law.

MARCUS
I should?

CHLOE
She needs comfort. You think she would prefer me or you?

MARCUS
But—? You don't mind—?

Chloe kisses him.

CHLOE
What can be wrong about comfort?

MARCUS
Well...

CHLOE
I need to grant a wish.

MARCUS
If you're sure...

CHLOE
Go on. You'll be back.

MARCUS
Well. Chloe, you are—

CHLOE
No gratitude. Just go.

> *He hesitates, then collects a blanket and crosses to Daphne and sits with her. Under the following scene she moves to grief to complaint to resting against him to necking with him.*

MIKE
You did this last summer?

OTTO
Last summer, no. Last year I was ill. But I have come out to see the Perseids almost every August since I was small.

> *Chloe puts on Daphne's hat. Gets blanket, crosses U of the wheelchair to Mike, who slaps a mosquito*

MIKE
Why bother, after the first time?

OTTO
"Why bother"? Why does the parent kiss the child goodnight each night, and not just once and be done with it? When the earth visits the Perseids, I like to step out and say hello. They were the beginning of my studies, and seeing them is like—is better than— seeing old friends.

MIKE
They are just balls of rock.

OTTO
That ring is just a ball of rock, no? But it means a great deal to you now.

Chloe is down on her knees, feeling around for the ring.

MIKE
If it's still on the ground in the morning, it's going to mean nothing at all to me. Zero. Nothing.

   He flails at a mosquito.

OTTO
When I was young and tasted better, the insects plagued me, as well. And there has been rain and wind and deep disappointment on Perseid nights. And my neck gets so sore...But they are friends; I cannot not care for them. They could throw a foolish glass of water in my face, and I would still admire them.

MIKE
I can't just take her back! Not after a fight like that!

OTTO
And if she comes back?

MIKE
That's as likely as—

   Chloe, still kneeling, takes his left hand.

MIKE
Oh!

OTTO
Did you see one?

MIKE
No, I—I thought perhaps—

> *Chloe puts the ring in his hand. He transfers it to his right hand and brings it up close to his eye. She gently kisses his left hand.*

MIKE
I—yes, I do see one.

OTTO
Where was it?

MIKE
Umm—straight ahead of me.

OTTO
Perhaps your eyes are getting used to the night.

MIKE
I could get used to this.

> *He feels at the baseball cap.*

MIKE
But it's so untypical...

Choloe slides up his body until she's standing, puts a finger to his lips, then embraces him.

OTTO
Only to you. The Perseids have been orbiting the sun for—how long? How could one discover it? They have been about their

business, but you have not been looking. Now you begin to look.

MIKE
(to Chloe)
This is different.

OTTO
Exactly! Things are the same, and yet different. It is the dance of the universe, where nothing is where it was but all are in relationship. Objects move away; others are lost for a time; but all are connected, and most return.

DAPHNE
(responding to Marcus)
Ooh.

OTTO
Where? Did you see that, Michael?

MIKE
(kissing Chloe)
Mmm-mmph.

OTTO
Courage: there will be more.

> *Chloe and Mike sink down under their blanket. Marcus and Daphne are wrapped in theirs.*
> *The lights begin a slow fade, down to just enough light on Otto for him to be seen as a blur by his last line.*

OTTO
I believe I come back to this field, year after year, because I am afraid. I am afraid. I am afraid because there was once a moment when I began to understand this great dance, this music that is so grand you can live out your life between one beat and the next. Of

this music, if your are granted it, you may hear a whole bar—only a few notes—and are they from the overture or from some point much later? Much closer to the end? And from this one bar we feel a need to extrapolate the whole symphony.

CHLOE
More...

OTTO
We have only what we are given, and for "more" we have to dream.

DAPHNE
Oh, more...

OTTO
And there was a moment when my dream began to show me the shape of the dance, the music. But then I was ill, and now I understand no more.

MARCUS
(to Daphne)
Do you want to?

OTTO
Who would not want to? I tried to continue to work, to connect with my colleagues, but even when they talked to me of theories I myself had put forward, I could not understand them any more. It is too painful, for many of them were my students, were my followers. Oh, there's a big one!

DAPHNE
There certainly is.

OTTO
So grand and bright, and so suddenly gone. But there are always more.

MIKE
More.

OTTO
The universe is not cold and still and dark. It is bright and resounding and rambunctious in its dance. It is we who must struggle to escape coldness and the dark.

CHLOE
It's so hot.

OTTO
I cannot understand my colleagues any more. I cannot understand my family, as they partner and shift and partner again. But once I understood the edge of the dance of the whole universe. I really did.

MARCUS and MIKE
Ohh.

OTTO
But now it is not necessary to understand, perhaps. The dance goes on, and in some small way, even in this field, we are part of it.

CHLOE
Mmmm.

OTTO
It is enough to remark it, to celebrate it, to salute it. To say Oh! at the bright night sky.

CHLOE and MARCUS Ohhh.

OTTO
(Of the sky)
Oh! Another nice one.

DAPHNE and MIKE
Nice...

OTTO
You will say "nice" is not a scientific term.

CHLOE and MARCUS
Nice...

OTTO
But it is a good word for a night when the sky dances for us, and we do not need to understand. Do you see how they dance? There is one.

THE OTHERS
Yes...

OTTO
(pointing) And another.

THE OTHERS
Ohhh. More...

OTTO
On a night like this, one can believe there will always be more.

Blackout

Curtain Call

Andrew Wetmore

About the author

Andrew Wetmore trained as a performer, but concluded relatively early that his skills did not match his enthusiasm in a way that would support a professional acting career. Instead, he has spent decades working with community theatres and regional playwrights. He was the founding chairperson of Dramatists' Co-op, an initiative by the Writers' Federation of Nova Scotia to improve the quality and increase the visibility of Nova Scotia-written scripts. For many years he was artistic director of Moveable Feast Theater, which performed in Quebec and Massachusetts. He founded and coordinated MVP (Merrimack Valley Playwrights), where writers in northern Massachusetts could hear trained actors read their scripts and get constructive feedback from their writing and acting colleagues.

Wetmore was born in Nova Scotia, and has returned to the province after many years 'down the road.' He is the editor for Moose House Publications, and for the infrastructure team of the Apache Software Foundation.

www.ingramcontent.com/pod-product-compliance
Lightning Source LLC
Chambersburg PA
CBHW071149120626
46546CB00006B/2192